PRIMETIME
Network Television Programming

PRIMETIME
Network Television Programming

Richard A. Blum • Richard D. Lindheim

Focal Press
Boston   London

Focal Press is an imprint of Butterworth Publishers.

Library of Congress Cataloging-in-Publication Data

Blum, Richard A.
  Primetime: network television programming.

  Bibliography: p.
  Includes index.
  1. Television programs.   I. Lindheim, Richard D.
II. Title.   III. Title: Prime time.
PN1992.55.B58   1987   384.55′44′0973   87-328
ISBN 0-240-51756-3

Butterworth Publishers
80 Montvale Avenue
Stoneham, MA 02180

10   9   8   7   6   5   4   3   2   1

Printed in the United States of America

To Elaine, Susan, and David; Jason and Jennifer.

Contents

Acknowledgments

The authors wish to acknowledge and thank the many people who have supported and contributed to this text. At the networks, studios, and in academia, we encountered the enthusiastic and generous cooperation of our professional colleagues. We appreciate all the suggestions, advice, and assistance in the preparation of our manuscript.

We would particularly like to thank Bill Hamm at Universal Television for his diligence in locating and identifying artwork and photographs and in securing clearances from various departments at the studios and networks.

We are grateful to Arlyn Powell, Editor for Focal Press, and his staff at Focal Press for their unwavering commitment and interest in this book.

Some people are innately gifted in their ability to inspire others. Norman Tamarkin is one such individual; his talent is greatly appreciated, respected, and admired. Friends are heavily relied upon in the long stages of writing. Frank Tavares has been particularly supportive in this effort as in others.

For their support throughout the long hours required for preparation of the manuscript, and their forbearance of the cost, cussing, and monopolizing of the telephone as we learned to conquer long-distance computer communication via modem, we would like to thank our understanding and compassionate families: Elaine, Susan, and David Lindheim; and Jason and Jennifer Blum. And for extended family support: Eve, Al, and Stephen Blum.

Finally, both of us must thank the students of the television courses we have taught and visited, who helped us gauge the interests, concerns, and needs of new talent in the television industry. We hope this book provides insightful information to fulfill those needs. In the process, we hope you, the reader, will benefit from this exploration into primetime television programming.

For permission to use copyrighted material, photographs, memos, and sample concepts and scripts, the authors gratefully acknowledge the following: At Universal Television: Nancy Cushing Jones, Lauri Rodich, Corinne DeLuca, Nancy Paciolla. At Warner Brothers Television: Milton Segal, Don Seldgreber, David Himmelfarb. At ABC/Cap Cities Broadcasting: Candace Farrell, Norma Herron, Ken Park. At Creative Artists Agency: Ron Meyer. At McCartt, Orek, and Barrett Agency: Bettye McCartt.

PRIMETIME
Network Television Programming

1

Introduction to Programming

Primetime television programming is the central, and perhaps the most competitive, activity in American broadcasting. It involves and affects everyone—creators (writers, producers, actors), buyers (network executives, advertisers), and, of course, the viewing public.

On the creative side, producers struggle to interest networks in new program concepts, while networks battle among themselves to win viewer loyalty. A network executive might sift through a thousand program concepts each year, commit to about a hundred scripts, and select about twenty for pilot production. Only a handful of those are scheduled as series. Of those, only one may return for a second season.

Despite the staggering odds against success, each season finds producers developing new shows and networks selecting a lucky few for scheduling. The viewer, who might be familiar with specific nightly schedules, suddenly finds the programming pattern interrupted to make room for specials, new shows, or old shows in new time slots. The number of viewers attracted to a specific time slot has a direct bearing on the cost per minute charged to advertisers. According to J.W. Thompson, USA, a leading advertising agency, advertisers spend more than $8 billion annually on television advertising. The loss of one rating point averaged over a primetime season can be worth $90 million.*

Programming decisions are obviously not made lightly. Over the years, certain strategies and principles help guide the selection process. Like a war game, those strategies sometimes pay off with historic success

*"Nielsen Ratings May Be Axed By Networks," *Washington Post*, 18 January 1987, H-8.

and at other times are tantamount to the death of the entire program schedule.

DEFINING PROGRAMMING

Programming is a concept that refers to different aspects of television viewing. For the public, it is the wealth of material available for viewing each night, with its inherent variety or perceived sameness. Television offers a range of material, with different stations competing for viewer attention. The program formats are broad: comedy series, dramatic or action series, movies of the week, specials, miniseries, children's programming, sports, and news. The choice is the viewer's—including turning to another station, renting a videocassette, or turning off the television set entirely.

For a television professional working at a network, a local station, or a cable television company, the concept of programming takes on a more immediate working definition. It is a two-pronged approach: finding and developing new shows that will attract the most appropriate audience, and scheduling shows on the air to compete effectively against all competition.

Executives at the network or station level worry about the same thing: attracting audiences to the station with the best scheduling of shows for particular *dayparts*. A daypart is a period of time analogous to viewer activities during the day. Mornings find the schedule filled with programming for young children and adults who do not work outside the home; afternoons are ripe for soap operas. Evening is "prime time" for family and adult viewing. Late-night offers appropriate scheduling for adults and inveterate insomniacs.

Primetime is, by far, the most critical daypart for a network. It consists of the hours from 8 P.M. to 11 P.M. Monday through Saturday, and 7 P.M. to 11 P.M. Sunday. This period represents the largest potential for audience viewing and the greatest opportunity to compete with other networks for national viewing supremacy. Some advertisers are concerned about reaching the largest audience, regardless of the demographic composition of that audience (that raw size is called *tonnage*). Other advertisers seek a specific viewing audience for their products, targeted to specific demographics.

Throughout the world, there is unmatched interest in American primetime programs. They are known and enjoyed by viewers in every part of the globe, and they are the lifeblood of television professionals at home.

HISTORIC OVERVIEW OF TV PROGRAMMING

Audience interest in program genres changes with the times, but programming appeal can be tracked and measured in relatively concrete terms.* Back in the 1950s, during the "Golden Age of Television," live comedy and drama graced the screen (_Texaco Star Theater, Fireside Theatre, Philco TV Playhouse, Your Show of Shows, Robert Montgomery Presents, Matinee Theater, The Colgate Comedy Hour, The Red Buttons Show_). When production moved from New York to California and prerecording on videotape became a reality, interest in live comedy and drama declined.

The Western was one of the new programming winners. Hollywood cowboys won the hearts of American viewers in the late 1950s and early 1960s. In 1960 alone, thirty-two Westerns were scheduled on the three networks. The following year, Westerns (_Wagon Train, Bonanza,_ and _Gunsmoke_) held the top three spots throughout the ratings season. Other programming formats emerged strong in the 1960s, including superspy action (_The Man from U.N.C.L.E., I Spy_) and satirical comedy (_That Was the Week That Was, Rowan & Martin's Laugh-In_).

Variety suggested that Americans' viewing tastes changed after 1968, when the country was agonizing over Vietnam and many social issues were raised in the public consciousness. Accordingly, the postwar baby boomers were no longer riveted to their television sets. The networks still had a vast array of viewers, but advertisers now wanted to bring back more baby boomers to see their shows. Programmers wanted desperately to appeal to the target demographics of young married and upwardly mobile professionals. As a result, primetime television tentatively embraced more controversial and serious themes for both comedy and drama. Norman Lear's _All in the Family_ was the forerunner of socially relevant comedy series, along with the ever−popular _M*A*S*H._**

Throughout the 1970s and 1980s, hard-hitting, realistic series and television films tried to make themselves appealing to the targeted

---

*For historical information on television programming see works such as Erik Barnouw, _Tube of Plenty: The Evolution of American Television_ (New York: Oxford University Press, 1982), Les Brown, _Encyclopedia of Television_ (New York: Zoetrope, 1982), Charles Clift, III and Archie Greer, eds., _Broadcasting Programming: The Current Perspective_ (Washington, D.C : University Press of America, annual), Lawrence W. Lichty and Malachi C. Topping, _American Broadcasting: A Source Book on the History of Radio and Television_ (New York: Hastings House, 1975). For additional resources on the history of television programming, see _Annoted Bibliography_.

**"Programming Takes Cue From Decades in Motion Following World War II," _Variety_, 4 June 1986, 57, 80.

demographic (sex and age composition of the television audience). Movies made for television confronted front-page topics such as nuclear proliferation, child abuse, wife abuse, homosexuality, and the homeless. The viewing public watched, and the networks eventually felt more comfortable developing, scheduling, and promoting issue-oriented television films.

Action series also became more realistic and gritty, as is evidenced by *The Equalizer, Hill Street Blues, Miami Vice,* and *St. Elsewhere.* The tone and style of the shows became more natural and the content more topical. Meanwhile, comedy series now touched the lives of ordinary people in recognizable situations. Consider the identifiable character conflicts in *Family Ties, Cheers,* and *The Golden Girls.* Perhaps *The Cosby Show* epitomizes the appeal of recognizable settings and characters played by identifiable stars. Featuring Bill Cosby as a doctor and his wife (played by Felicia Rashad) as a lawyer, this family comedy became the runaway ratings hit of the 1985–1986 television season.

Programming genres are constantly evolving, along with the interests of the viewing audience. In an interview celebrating NBC's sixtieth anniversary, Grant Tinker, then chairman of NBC, observed that there are now multiple seasons to the television program cycle and that "program popularity changes are strictly cyclical. Sitcoms are almost saturated now. On the other hand, Westerns and variety shows seem to be entirely a thing of the past. There's no hope for those. If you put them on, no one will watch."* Tinker predicted that primetime magazine programming might play a significant role in the future and encouraged the development of shows such as *1986.* This is a less expensive form of programming, something that has become a forced reality for the networks.

Brandon Tartikoff, president of NBC's entertainment division, reaffirmed those views.** In assessing the 1986 primetime programming schedule, he noted that while situation comedies were almost dead a few years ago, they have reemerged with a vengeance, resulting in a barrage of comedies on all the networks. He observed that serials are "trending down" and that dramatic miniseries will continue ("it's still the most distinctive service we can provide"). Topical television films are also a mainstay, as he noted, "Producers can get a story on the screen in four to five months after the fact, while feature films take at least 18 months." Obviously, this type of programming is expensive to produce. As of 1986, the average network license fee for a one-hour program was $850,000; the fee for a half-hour show was $350,000. The producers must finance the rest of the production costs independently. As a result,

*"Grant Tinker: The Master of the Medium," *Variety*, 4 June 1986, 56.

**"Brandon Tartikoff: The Winner & New Champ," *Variety*, 4 June 1986, 58.

Tartikoff said that networks will begin to rely on less expensive magazine shows such as *1986* and *West 57th*, "so we can afford action hours and high-ticket made—for—tv movies and miniseries."*

When Grant Tinker left NBC to form his own production company in 1987 (T/G Productions with Gannett Company), the highly praised series *1986* was cancelled. According to NBC News President Lawrence Grossman, the cancellation permitted a new programming emphasis for the network—documentaries that explore major issues behind the news.**

The historical ebb and flow of programming genres seems to mesh with network needs and public expectations. One television critic recently argued that programming genres constantly reappear in different forms, appearing fresh to contemporary audiences.*** The program incentive is to reach the widest possible home viewing audience.

Despite the inroads of cable, pay television, and home videos, network primetime television remains the United States' primary source of home entertainment, attracting millions of viewers to the latest offerings. The networks' ability to reach audiences is unmatched, and for that reason, the battleground is set for intense competition between creators and networks.

PROGRAMMING PRINCIPLES

Television programming is a dynamic business, with an intricate mix of buyers and sellers. Independent producers and major studios are in a constant battle for network commitments in script development, pilot production, and full series purchases. Once these formidable hurdles are passed, final arguments are advanced by all sides for optimum network time slots. All the players know that a promising series in the wrong time slot might not survive its first season.

To help reach informed decisions, network executives rely on certain resources, tools, and strategies that have proved invaluable over the years. Among their programming concerns are network competition, audience research, and scheduling.

Network Seasons

Traditionally, television executives programmed for a few distinct seasons: the fall premiere season, the winter second season, spring

---

*"Brandon, Tartikoff: The Winner & New Champ," *Variety*, 4 June 1986, 58.

**"Grossman Looks at NBC News Future," *Broadcasting*, 12 January 1987, 132.

***"Gone Today, Here Tomorrow: Show Genres May Fade Away But Can Rise From the Grave," *Variety*, 14 January 1987, 142.

tryouts for new short-run series, and summer reruns and pilots that never made it to series. Those distinct seasons (which had their own ratings evaluations, or sweeps) have gradually blended into one continuous season, however, and the networks can introduce new shows at any time of the year.

The most important programming cycles are still the *sweeps*. Four times a year the two major audience measurement firms—the A.C. Nielsen Company and the American Research Bureau—gather data nationwide to measure the shows in every television market across the country. During this time, the networks try to bolster their schedules with strong movies, specials, and other programming stunts.

Audience Research

Audience research is a primary resource for any network or station programmer. Research can be categorized as *quantitative* or *qualitative*. The former is objective information about numbers and viewers (for example, how many people are watching at a given time). In contrast, qualitative research provides information about viewer attitudes (for instance, whether people like or dislike what they see).

The most widely known research firm, A.C. Nielsen, provides a wide variety of data services. For example, the *overnights* provide raw data about program reach in twelve major cities (total numbers of viewers, not categorized by age or sex). The *MNAs* (Multi Network Area Report) detail ratings performance in seventy of the most populous cities with at least three commercial television stations. The *Pocketpiece* is a detailed summary of national findings, analyzing the performance of shows competitively, with program ratings, shares, and information about audience size and composition.

The Nielsen measurements have traditionally relied on about seventeen hundred household meters (*Audimeters*) and about two thousand household diaries to provide their analysis. Subscribing to that system cost the networks $3.5 million annually. After thirty years, that system was scheduled to be superseded in the 1987-1988 television season by the electronic *people meter*. The new system offers an integrated service. Using an electronic remote control device, family members indicate when they are watching the TV and when they are not. These data can then be ascertained on a daily basis and correlated with the traditional rating and share household information. Advertising agencies and the companies they represent agreed that the new system would be more accurate and accessible than the old technique. However, in preliminary concurrent tests, people-meter data differed substantially from the traditional N.T.I. (national) reports. These differences were greatest among ratings for children, where 20 percent discrepancies were found on shows like _The Cosby Show_. The rating differences were great enough to affect the ranking of shows in the early morning and daytime programming periods. Since the networks could lose significant advertising revenue if ratings were proven to be lower, they vigorously debated the accuracy of the new system and demanded special studies be undertaken to verify the discrepancies. As a result the introduction of the people meter system was postponed one year—from September 1, 1986 to September 1, 1987. With the new system still controversial in January, 1987, ABC decided not to use A.C. Nielsen's service, CBS signed up with Nielsen's competitor (AGB Television Research, Inc.), and NBC was still debating its options. Nielsen hoped to attract the networks back after some further testing of the system.*

Ratings and shares are important measurements of a show's reach. A _rating_ is a percentage of viewership based on the total number of television homes in the United States. A _share_ is a percentage of viewership based on the number of homes using television at the time. Consequently, a late-night show might receive a very low rating (many people are asleep at that hour) but a very high share (those watching television at that time clearly preferred that show).

To supplement the quantitative measurements, other research methods specialize in qualitative information. For example, _TVQs_ examine the popularity and familiarity of certain shows and performers. ASI Market Research measures audience reactions to concepts, pilots, and series episodes.

Another variation of qualitative research is the _vulnerability study_, which measures the competitive strengths of different shows on the air. It asks the viewer to indicate a preference: "If these shows were on at the same time, which would you select?"

The key to successful use of research lies in the programmer's ability to interpret and bolster his or her own programming strategies. Brandon Tartikoff, Harvey Shephard (former head of programming at CBS), and others stress that "research is very much a service to the programming department rather than an enemy."** Programs are tested from concept to pilot, but the programming executives must make the final judgment.

Examples of how Tartikoff uses research were illustrated in a _Variety_ interview***: "All of us in the program department were lukewarm to _Highway to Heaven_ until the research people came in and said it was the highest pilot they ever tested." They decided to schedule the

---

*"Nielsen Ratings May Be Axed By Networks," _Washington Post_, 18 January 1987, Business Section, H 1, 8-9.

**"Brandon Tartikoff: The Winner & New Champ," _Variety_, 4 June 1986, 58.

***IBID.

show despite their own misgivings, and the ratings took off. One of the lowest tested shows for that same season was *Miami Vice*. "But it was the collective feeling of all of us that it would work. So we went for it." The research was used as a base for evaluating program strength, but it was not the sole and exclusive arbiter of judgment.*

Programming Strategies

Program executives rely on several basic strategies to beat the competition. They carefully analyze the current schedule and might decide to use *counter programming* strategy—that is, schedule shows with contrasting appeal to win uncommitted viewers. For example, a major sports spectacular might draw a huge, predominantly male audience to one network, while another network airs a show with particular appeal to women at the same time. Another strategy is *competitive programming*—that is, airing shows to compete head-on for audiences. A perfect example is NBC's 1986 decision to move *Miami Vice* so that it competed directly against *Dallas*.

After analyzing the program schedule, the programmer might decide that the best strategy lies in *block programming*, or airing similar types of programs in a string to take advantage of audience flow. To maximize that effect, several comedy or adventure shows might air back-to-back. The strategy is to encourage the audience to stay with the network throughout the night.

One way of gauging the effective placement of shows is to look at the strengths and weaknesses of the show preceding (*lead-in*) and following (*lead-out*) specific programs. A programmer will want to start the evening with a strong lead-in to build viewer interest in the ensuing program blocks.

The placement of a new show in the schedule can make or break the series. Usually a new show will benefit from the preestablished appeal of surrounding shows. For that reason, programmers often try to place a new show in a *hammock* slot. A new comedy series might be positioned between two well-established comedies. Once the new series gains an audience of its own, the hammock slot can be relinquished to another show. A reverse strategy is called *tentpoling*. In this case, a strong, established program is placed between two new shows or shows with weak ratings to help attract a larger audience.

Once a program schedule is set, the programmer can still come up with unusual events to attract a one-time audience, particularly during sweeps. The term *stunting* refers to this strategy of shifting programs,

_____

*"Brandon Tartikoff: The Winner & New Champ," *Variety*, 4 June 1986, 58.

scheduling specials, using an extended-format introduction of series (a one-hour special for a half-hour series), and arranging casting crossovers between shows. The idea is to attract audiences with heavy promotional gambits.

No matter what the strategy, the aim is the same: to win the audience and beat the competition.

THIS BOOK'S APPROACH TO PROGRAMMING

This book provides a model of network primetime programming activities, analyzing the principles, strategies, and theories of program development, production, and scheduling. These principles can be applied to every other form of programming in the television industry.

The quintessential activities of television programming can be categorized into three interrelated areas: creating, selling, and buying. This book deals with the specific roles of creators, sellers, and buyers in every phase of primetime television programming, from concept development and production to network scheduling and cancellation. Since television is a collaborative medium, it is important to know the roles played by all those people involved in the process. The authors' intent is to provide a clear blueprint of who is responsible for what in the primetime programming paradigm.

Part I looks at the personnel structure of the television industry. It introduces the key members of the creative team—actors, writers, and producers. We look at their roles in the development and production process and discuss career training relevant to these positions.

The buyer's side of the equation also is explored, focusing on management roles in a network hierarchy. We include a detailed analysis of key management positions, from the network president to heads of various program divisions. Also included are specific job responsibilities for managers of primetime comedy and drama series, miniseries, television movies, network-originated productions, specials, daytime shows, and children's programming. Additionally, one section details the most common professional training for network management positions.

Sellers of primetime television have their own hierarchies and diverse responsibilities. Most new ideas come to the network through independent producers, major studios, and agents or packagers. Profiles of these channels are provided, including an exploration of some of the most powerful creators in the industry.

Part II looks at the creative process of developing new shows, critical to an understanding of the television industry. Where do new ideas come from? How are they developed into successful presentations? This part examines the strategies and techniques involved in translating original concepts into effective series presentations. We look at sample concepts and analyze the importance of series settings, characters, and sample stories. A typical network pitch session is described, and ingredients for success are defined.

Creative techniques are essential in developing effective pilot stories and scripts. One section examines techniques for writing effective concepts, pilot stories, and scripts. Plot development is explored, as is characterization, along with the tools for evaluating credible characters. To serve as models of format and style, script excerpts are provided from pilots of *Murder, She Wrote* and *Miami Vice*.

Networks often are ambivalent about the effectiveness of pilots versus other forms of series presentations; all sides of this issue are presented. We also investigate the perennial conflict over network approval rights. In this section, we show how networks evaluate lead actors (a sample casting session is described), directors, pilot script revisions, and broadcast standards compliance.

Once a network commits to production of a pilot or series, a new phase emerges, requiring the talents and expertise of many creative, technical, and management teams. The special roles played by key people in the production process are defined, and the entire production effort is covered, from scheduling and budgeting to postproduction.

Throughout our discussion, a distinctive perspective is maintained: the interlocking interests of creators, sellers, and buyers. We look at techniques used to develop and produce new comedy and drama series. We also identify the criteria used by network managers to evaluate new projects at every phase.

Two particularly strong influences on network decisions are audience testing techniques and network scheduling practices. Network executives analyze time slots, with detailed information about the performance of current and competing shows. Armed with recommendations from program researchers, and using traditional programming strategies, they reach critical decisions about scheduling strategy.

Once a show is on the air, its performance falls under the aegis of current programming. This division is responsible for maintaining the strength of all ongoing series. In Part III, the role of current programming executives at studios and networks is discussed. Specific functions are explained, including reviews of series scripts, rough cuts, and scheduling. Many programming options and strategies are available to the network and studio. In this section, we explore programming techniques and strategies that help determine what gets on the air, what gets moved, and what gets canceled.

Part IV looks at the development of programs intended for a single broadcast, as opposed to long-term series. This section examines the special requirements of creating, producing, and scheduling these popular network forms: miniseries, television movies, and specials. We look at the genesis of ideas and examine sample promotional campaigns for large-scale projects such as "Winds of War," "The Thorn Birds," and "The Day After." Although network news specials and live sporting events might fit into the specials category, our emphasis is on the entertainment form, as this is by far the most common format in non-series network programming.

Part V looks at the pragmatic issues of creative constraints, as well as business concerns. The creator generally finds a number of internal and external constraints imposed on all television shows. These come in the form of reactions from the broadcast standards and practices division, as well as from external pressure groups monitoring program content for various reasons. This section looks at the delicate balance between creating programs and being sensitive to pressure group concerns.

A subsequent chapter reviews the business aspects of primetime television. No shows could be produced without business and legal counsel to negotiate and close business deals. The networks and studios have their own business executives and legal counsel for this purpose. One of the most important agreements is a license fee, negotiated between the producer and the network. The terms and ramifications of these agreements are far-reaching, tapping into the potential wellspring of profits in syndication and other markets.

Finally, Part VI looks at the historical trends in network programming and possibilities for the future. This section discusses the evolution of the networks, the factors contributing to change, and the impact of new technology on television programming.

An appendix and annotated bibliography are included to provide further resource material on all topics covered in this book.

The authors hope that through this exploration of primetime programming activities, you will gain a better understanding of the practical and collaborative nature of television programming. Creators develop myriad new shows; networks buy a limited number to bolster faltering time slots. The industry thrives on symbiotic skills, talents, and knowledge.

If your career engages you in a creative or management position, the authors hope you can use some of the ideas in this book to help you influence the direction of television programming.

Creating, Buying, and Selling: The Personnel Structure of the Television Industry

The cast and crew prepare for a scene in *Miami Vice*. Shown in the foreground are actor Philip Michael Thomas (left) and director Paul Michael Glaser (right).

The Creative Team

In television, the creative community is generally responsible for coming up with new ideas for programs. That community is comprised of actors, writers, and producers. Creators and management interact at almost every level of development, with specific and sometimes overlapping responsibilities. Creators might develop new concepts and proposals, while management might package the project for strategic marketing purposes.

A show can be conceived with or without management involvement, but its formal development rests almost exclusively in the talents of the actors, writers, and independent producers. This chapter will look at the roles creators play in the primetime programming process.

ACTORS

In the realm of new programming, it is not unusual for a star to formulate the idea for a new series, special, or movie of the week. The performer might be so popular that he or she has a contractual arrangement with the network to star in a new show, and sometimes to produce or direct one. The preestablished audience appeal of such a performer is enticing to the network because it seems to ensure success. But an analysis of the track record of such series proves otherwise. A star does not necessarily heighten the prospects of a show's success.

Leading actors who have a strong TVQ (a controversial test measure of popularity with audiences) have a relatively powerful hand in negotiating new programming options. Like their celestial namesakes, however, stars are subject to meteoric rises and falls. Even the most famous are subject to the erratic nature of public acclaim. The list of popular performers who have failed to carry a series includes stellar names such as Alan Alda, James Stewart, Lindsay Wagner, Rock Hudson, Karl Malden, and Loni Anderson. Still, the appeal of stars such as Bill Cosby occasionally transcends the medium.

A strong TVQ attests to the actor's current ability to attract wide audiences for program sponsors, and that factor is crucial in the casting of movies, miniseries, and specials, which are scheduled for one-time viewing to attract high ratings.

Regardless of the format, the television star is likely to be typecast in familiar roles. Comedy stars are not likely to be action heroes, while dramatic leads are not likely to be slapstick comedians. If you look at actors in the current television season, you probably will notice a repetitive pattern to some of their roles and performances. Audiences expect them to be in certain types of roles and would be disappointed if they did not appear in those roles. It may be a new show, but a familiar multi-million-dollar hero is in the driver's seat.

What makes an actor star material? There is no surefire way to success, even with the best press agent working to create a star image. Some actors seem to possess personal magnetism that leaps from the television screen into the living room. They have the intangible gift of charisma. All actors strive to make their roles credible and identifiable, but somehow the primetime star conveys a personality type that is emotionally charged and is welcome in the homes of millions of viewers each night.

Amiability is more important than many people realize. While the ranks of movie stars contain many individuals who earned stardom playing cold, fearless, tough characters, the track record for such individuals on television is not very good. The most common television star is warm, outgoing, and likable. In research, he or she often is described as someone the viewer would like to have as a friend. Even Archie Bunker, the laughable bigot of *All in the Family*, appealed to audiences because of his emotional susceptibility. It is interesting to speculate whether Humphrey Bogart, the penultimate tough guy of cinema, would have become a star on television.

Another personality dimension common to many television stars is that they tend to be emotional, volatile, and passionate—as opposed to cool, collected, and intellectual. Perhaps we like "hot" personalities because they hold our attention, even as we sit in our living rooms, where we are easily distracted.

Consistency Is the Key in Role Preparation and Performance

Actors approach their roles from an emotional, physical, or intellectual core. The actor's approach to a role distinguishes his or her performance style. When an actor is cast in a part, he or she undertakes an extensive preparation period. The script is analyzed according to dramatic beats, psychological motivations, character objectives, the character's sense of urgency, the dramatic or comedic conflicts, and the behavior and thoughts of the character in each given circumstance of the show. The actor interprets not only the emotional aspects of the performance but also its intellectual and physical elements.

During the rehearsal period, the director might have a different interpretation of the characters and their interrelationships. The actors and the director work together to find the right approach. In television, rehearsal time is extremely limited in comparison to that in film and theater. The schedule is particularly grueling in a primetime series, where the principals often work ten to twelve hours a day. Actors work long periods without a break, and the revised script for the next day's shooting might arrive at midnight, giving them little time to prepare for any changes.

During the actual production process, the script is shot out of sequence, with many repetitive "takes" of very short scenes. On location or in the studio, scenes might be shot for close-ups, wide shots, reaction shots, and over-the-shoulder shots, all of which will be edited later. In addition to the discontinuous nature of scene progression, actors must contend with repetitive takes for each scene and the practicalities of camera blocking. It is essential to hit the mark at all times, or the actor will be out of focus, out of frame, or out of the light. Actors must, therefore, maintain psychological, physical, and vocal consistency at different points in the day. It is somewhat remarkable that the end result appears consistent, believable, spontaneous, and natural.

Once the show is edited, actors are called onto the dubbing and looping stage for the final phase. Here they provide voice-overs, correct earlier dialogue problems, reinterpret line deliveries, and clarify lines that might have been lost due to noise on the set. They listen to their original dialogue on headsets while watching their performance on a screen, and they try to provide an interpretive consistency in their lines.

Figure 2–1.   Actress Season Hubley prepares for a scene in *Alfred Hitchcock Presents.*

Training Grounds for Actors

Creating the semblance of spontaneity and dimensionality is critical to good acting. Where do actors learn these skills? Many primetime television actors get experience dealing with the constraints of the medium through daytime soap operas, which have the same time and technical constraints. Commercials might appear to be another training ground, but few primetime actors actually come from that arena.

Many television and film actors acquire experience on the stage. Professional schools and workshops concentrate on creative growth, using *inner* and *outer* techniques. Actors learn how to approach a script and interpret characters and dialogue (inner work); they also learn blocking and physical action (outer technique). They concentrate on consistency, pacing and style, and working with directors and other actors to achieve the most unified and powerful performance.

WRITERS

All new program concepts must be written—a fact that many people take for granted. Whether it is a pilot for a new series, a movie of the week, a miniseries, or a television special, the premise must be fleshed out and presented in appropriate form by a television writer. The process writers go through to get a show on the air is analogous to a war game: Ideas are constantly being written and rewritten in an attempt to second-guess the buyer in the marketplace. In the collaborative medium of television, writing means rewriting.

Writers who create new series proposals play by the rules of the game. Network program heads may give speeches about innovative programming, but they buy just the opposite. Experienced writers have learned that familiar formulas are more salable than new, untested ideas. New program ideas stand the best chance of interesting buyers only if they are reminiscent of other successes. A writer can create intriguing new premises, rich with characters and plots, but the basic format must remain within the context of successful television programming.

The series concept is written in a form that merges creative ideas with the pragmatics of industry needs. The proposal introduces the buyer to the basic format, characters, and pilot story. The pilot story shows how characters behave in dramatic or comedic conflicts and how they interact with each other. The series presentation also offers a sampling of future episodes to show the longevity of the series concept. If the project is a miniseries or multipart television film, the writer creates a _bible_ to sell it. The series bible provides a historical overview of the dramatic narrative and might include the complete pilot teleplay. It is an important selling device, showing in great detail how the stories and characters will be handled in the series.

Television is a collaborative medium, but the story and script that finally emerge are the foundation on which the production is built. A dramatic or comic story must be told within a prescribed act structure of 30, 60, 90, or 120 minutes. Generally, the television story begins with a teaser to attract audience interest and builds action throughout each act. A good script involves viewers in the characters' lives and conflicts. Well-written projects have a gripping plot, with strong pacing and clever builds. Characters seem real in action, reaction, and dialogue. A weak script will be exposed by boring and static scenes, predictable situations, cliché-ridden dialogue, inconsistent characters, erratic action, and too many holes in the story line.

In any new series, producers meet regularly with the networks and pass along critical information to the story editor and writer. Story conferences are held on a regular basis to work out all the problems at various stages. The writer gets feedback in meetings with the producer and story editor. Rewriting and polishing continue until everyone is sure the work is in top form.

Writing Credits

Television credits are very important for financial and professional reasons. *Created by* means the writer conceived the idea and sold it to the buyer. Each time the show airs, he or she receives royalty and residual payments. *Written by* means the writer was commissioned to write the story and the script and is entitled to full royalties and residuals for that development effort. If the writer receives *story by* credit, it means he or she wrote the story, but someone else was hired to do the teleplay. Since the payment for writing a story is considerably less than for doing the script, royalties are scaled down accordingly. If another writer is hired to do the script, he or she gets *teleplay by* credit, along with fees for the script and appropriate royalties for that phase.

Within a production unit (the staff that produces a series), writers can receive any number of production titles, which can be very confusing. Titles for writers have become like billing for actors. A television series usually has an executive producer (who may be a writer), supervising producers, line producers, executive story consultants, story editors, and staff writers. Their exact function varies from show to show.

Often a story consultant or story editor is a writer who is in a supervisory position on the series. This person provides creative continuity for the series and knows exactly what the network wants in future stories and scripts. Story editors know whether dialogue is off, characters are consistent, or stories are redundant. If the network wants changes in characters, romantic twists in the story, or more identifiable heroes, the story editor conveys that information to the writers. Story editors often polish stories and scripts themselves. It is not unusual for a story editor to rewrite a script completely but receive no screen credit for doing so. Production demands also require script modifications, which are the responsibility of the staff writer.

Writers not affiliated with studios are called free-lancers. They can create ideas on spec (speculatively with no sure buyer) or on assignment (contracted to write the story or script). Free-lancers have little job security, even though script fees are high and they might receive multiple writing assignments. Free-lance writers who are under contract must be paid the going rates, established by the Writers Guild of America, regardless of whether a producer likes the work or not.

Training Grounds for Writers

Most story editors are former free-lance writers who trade the freedom of working on their own for the steady paycheck and heavy work load of a staff position. They might have written for several major series in their specialty: action adventure, comedy, or primetime soap. Daytime soap operas are an excellent training ground for staff writers, since the genre requires hordes of scripts and daily story conferences. Many television writers also have some background in writing fiction, which helps them structure plots and describe characters and visual settings. Playwriting is another good training ground; it provides a respect for the impact of dramatic structure on live audiences.

Television or film production is another relevant training ground. A writer who understands the potential of the medium is more likely to take full advantage of that potential in stories and scripts. A background in production offers a working knowledge of the realistic possibilities and limitations in a script. Writers who produce and direct are called _hyphenates_. Usually they begin their careers as writers, gain staff experience in production, and expand into producing or directing to retain control over their material.

PRODUCERS

The producer is responsible for every decision from preproduction through postproduction. Every artistic, technical, and management concern falls under this person's direction, including casting, story and script development, production planning and shooting, editing and pacing, dubbing, looping, and network relations. The overall look and feel of the series is in the hands of the producer.

Interestingly, the role of a producer differs greatly between television and feature films. In motion pictures, the producer might be an entrepreneur, responsible for business decisions connected with the film, including packaging top talent, finding financial backing, and securing distribution. The director is the one who seems to hold the most creative power. In fact, the _auteur theory_ holds that the director is the most important creative artist in film. That view belies the reality of a collaborative medium, but its persistence suggests the relative power associated with directing feature films as compared to television programs.

In television the roles are reversed. The producer provides the creative direction and oversees every element of program planning, casting, and production, having the final say on all creative content and artistic problems. In contrast, the director is hired to do one episode. Television directors shoot under an extremely tight schedule. They have seven days to prepare a one-hour show and eight days to shoot it. There is little time to match the creative input that can occur in a more loosely scheduled and lavishly budgeted motion picture project.

The artistic direction for a show and its ultimate success or failure is largely determined by the talents and expertise of those chosen by the producer. The story editor is one of the first to be employed. The associate producer, also at the top of the list, helps coordinate production efforts.

During the run of a series, the producer meets regularly with network executives to discuss reactions to every step of story development and the production process. In story conferences, he or she meets with the story editors, suggesting new ideas for episodes and making commitments for new stories and scripts.

Day-to-Day Duties

In addition to working on upcoming shows, a producer supervises every aspect of the show currently in production. During *dailies* (or *rushes*) the producer views the previous day's shooting in the screening room with the director, associate producer, story editors, and studio executives. The rushes are replays of all the takes and inserts shot by the camera operators. Discussions center on performance styles, scenes to be reshot, scenes to be *looped* (actors' dialogue needs replacement), and scenes that can be cut together.

A *rough cut* is the first time anyone sees the film cut together from fade-in to fade-out. A rough cut contains every scene shot and is long and slow paced. In rough-cut screenings, the producer determines what will be edited. He or she has specific recommendations concerning scene selection, cutting, rearrangement, and editorial pacing. After the editors have made these changes, another screening is scheduled with the producer, and more changes are dictated for proper running time. Once that cut is ready, a screening called *M and E* (*music and effects*) takes place. During this run, the producer decides the placement of music, dubbing (sound effects, such as wind, crickets, or a car screech, all balanced against the music track), and looping of the actors' lines. After the film has been dubbed with music and effects, the producer again views the show for *final cut* approval.

You can see why television is considered largely a producer's medium. Consistency, story flow, pacing, production quality, and overall success are dependent on his or her creative ability and supervisory skills. To accomplish these seemingly impossible tasks, a producer relies heavily on an experienced production unit that can deliver under pressure. To be a producer, you must get along with network and studio executives, agents, writers, story editors, directors, casting directors, actors, composers, conductors, editors, and the entire production crew.

Figure 2–2.   A producer relies on an experienced production unit to accomplish all the technical tasks.

Training Grounds for Producers

One of the steppingstones to producing is the position of associate producer, which in turn is achieved with lower-level production unit experience. Although there is no clear apprenticeship route, film or television production training is an obvious asset. Having on-line responsibilities for shows is essential in understanding the full range of options possible in program production.

Other producers come from the executive side of television, where decisions about the strengths and weaknesses of particular shows are made on a daily basis. A network or studio executive knows network requirements intricately, which is an asset in producing.

Agents sometimes end up as producers, after spending many years representing successful projects in the marketplace and packaging the most successful elements of highly rated primetime shows. Actors sometimes make their employment conditional on the fact that they receive producing credit for their own series or television films. Even if they have the title of producer, however, most actors rarely become actively involved in overseeing the production process.

3

The Buyers: Network Television Management

Network television is the predominant marketplace for major Hollywood-based production, and its programming permeates virtually every household in the United States. Yet it is a surprisingly small business. In comparison to corporate entities such as General Motors or IBM, the total number of network employees is miniscule. One studio, such as Universal, employs more people than NBC, CBS, or ABC. The total number of employees, excluding secretaries, who are involved in national programming decisions number slightly over one hundred for each network.

The network programming staff makes crucial decisions that determine the viewing options for millions of viewers and the producing options for independent producers. In this chapter, we will look at the roles and responsibilities of network programming executives and then examine practical training grounds for these management positions.

Each network has an entertainment division responsible for all national non-news programs in all dayparts. Other divisions of the network include news, corporate, sales, operations, and stations. It is the entertainment division that exclusively manages programming decisions for primetime television.

Following is a typical management configuration for a network entertainment division:

President

V.P. Primetime Programs

V.P. Comedy Development
V.P. Current Comedy Programs
V.P. Drama Development
V.P. Current Drama Programs
V.P. Miniseries
V.P. Television Movies

V.P. Production
V.P. Specials
V.P. Daytime
V.P. Children's Programs

What do all these people do? Each heads a department that is critical to the ongoing process of the development, production, and scheduling of new and current shows. Each executive has a small staff, generally comprised of a director, a manager, and appropriate support staff. Let us examine their roles in the network programming hierarchy.

PRESIDENT, ENTERTAINMENT DIVISION

The president of the entertainment division is responsible for all entertainment programs broadcast by the network. He or she sets the network's identifiable programming philosophy and determines the balance among movies, specials, and regular series. Similarly, he or she decides how many comedy and drama series appear in the programming lineup. Former network programmers Fred Silverman and Harvey Shephard are masters of scheduling. Good shows can wither and die, while marginal shows can become substantial successes, simply because of scheduling.

The head of the entertainment division approves all major programming projects, including miniseries. He or she works closely with the sales department to target network audience objectives. For example, CBS traditionally has attracted older audiences and people living in middle America. ABC, and more recently NBC, have targeted young, urban audiences as their main objective.

The entertainment president announces the new network schedule each spring and is the final arbiter on series ordered, canceled, or removed from the schedule. This key executive reports directly to the president of the network. It is important to note that broadcast standards and practices executives are considered corporate officers and do not report to the entertainment division; their top executive is on equal footing with the entertainment chief. This structure provides a system of checks and balances, with the president of the network serving as the final arbiter of disputes. In actuality, conflicts rarely reach this level; disagreements usually are resolved in plea-bargaining sessions between division heads.

Within the entertainment division, vice presidents of various day-parts and special operations report directly to the president. They head specific program areas such as primetime programs, miniseries, production, daytime programs, children's programs, and specials.

VICE PRESIDENTS

Primetime Programs

The vice president of primetime programs is responsible for the development and supervision of all primetime dramatic and comedy series. As head of the busiest programming area, a good working relationship with the president of the entertainment division is essential.

The head of primetime programs implements the programming philosophy of the network, directing subordinates to favor certain types of projects over others. In this regard, he or she also designates producers and writers most likely to deliver successful programming. This executive might pursue and sign the most competitive production talent for exclusive network contracts. In recent years, there have been such agreements between ABC and Aaron Spelling and between NBC and Gary Goldberg.

In everyday function, the head of series programming evaluates scripts in development recommended by subordinates. This person also reads special or problem scripts of ongoing series. In addition, he or she attends the taping of half-hour comedy pilots, screens unfinished film assemblages of pilots and important or problematic series episodes, and meets with series producers and writers to set the direction of each series.

On occasion, this executive meets with the development staff to brainstorm and target future areas of development. In these meetings, it is not unusual for network personnel to conceive a series premise and determine the producer or production entity most desired to implement the idea. A meeting with the chosen creative team follows, and the producer/writer might amend the idea or even reject it. If rejected, the network contacts another producer, repeating the same process. Sometimes, after being rejected a number of times, the network might abandon the concept. More often, the project moves forward, at least through the making of a pilot. Some examples of successful series developed this way are *The A-Team*, *Knight Rider*, *Hill Street Blues*, and *Miami Vice*.

The head of primetime programs oversees four important and distinct departments: comedy development, current comedy programs, drama development, and current drama programs. Each area is managed by a program executive at the vice-presidential level. These four key people report to the head of primetime programs, and each has a staff of directors and managers reporting to him or her.

Comedy Development

As the title implies, this individual is responsible for the development of new half-hour and hour comedies. Normally, at least one director and manager of comedy development report to the department head.

The development process begins with a series of meetings with comedy writers and producers, who orally present their ideas for new series. While the network executive might occasionally offer some suggestions and modifications, more often he or she either accepts or rejects the idea. Following the presentation, the head of comedy development, after consulting with subordinates, telephones the originator and declares the verdict: "pass" (which is tantamount to death of the idea) or "proceed." If the decision is positive, meetings follow to discuss the principal characters and the story line for the pilot episode. The writer is then dispatched to begin work.

The head of comedy development reads all pilot scripts. Weak or unsalvageable scripts are abandoned. Those that have promise are the subject of subsequent meetings, during which the script is criticized in detail and changes are suggested. Once again, the writer is sent away to revise the script. After reading second and final drafts of all scripts, the vice president of comedy development selects the projects with the greatest potential. These scripts are recommended for pilot production and given to the head of the entertainment division for evaluation.

A network usually develops between thirty and forty scripts each year and makes pilots for eight to ten of these. The vice president of comedy development participates in selecting the cast and director for each pilot, attends table readings and rehearsals (where more changes are made), and sits in the control booth with the director and other key people as the pilot is videotaped before a live audience. (Most situation comedies are videotaped, as opposed to being filmed.) Before production is completed, an unfinished version is shown to the comedy development executives for final suggestions, changes, and approval.

Current Comedy Programs

While development might appear to be the more glamorous and challenging job, maintaining returning series is the backbone of any network schedule. There is a direct relationship between the number of renewable series and the financial and ratings success of the network. The person in charge of current comedy programs supervises the performance of all returning comedy shows. He or she has a staff of directors and managers, each of whom usually supervises no more than three ongoing series.

The daily demands on the vice president of current comedy programs can be extremely rigorous. Not only must this person read each draft of each script for every series, but he or she also attends the table readings that precede the production of each episode. This executive or one of his or her subordinates attends the taping of each episode of every comedy series, a process that can take up to three hours per episode.

In addition to the rigors of the preproduction and production of each episode, the head of current comedy is concerned with the ratings of ongoing comedy series and maintaining a strong and appropriate national audience.

Drama Development

The dividing line between comedy and drama has become blurred in the past few years. Some of the best comedy programs have strong dramatic elements, and humor has become an important quotient in almost all dramatic programs. The conventional yardstick used to differentiate comedy and drama has been length; a comedy is generally one-half hour, while a drama is an hour or more. But even that distinction has been breached. One successful hour show, *Crazy Like a Fox*, was developed by the comedy department of CBS, and drama departments are actively reexploring the half-hour form, which dominated the early days of television.

With these deviations in mind, it is safe to define drama programs as those in which the dramatic structure predominates and the show lasts one hour or more. In addition, with rare exceptions, drama shows are produced on 35mm film, much like motion pictures.

The working activity of the vice president of drama development closely parallels that of his or her counterpart in comedy. Potential development projects are orally presented by writers and producers. Those concepts selected for consideration are the topic of extensive discussions about characters and pilot stories. The vice president reads all scripts, including the first and second drafts, commenting on and evaluating every element and finally approving selected scripts for pilot production. This key executive is closely involved in selecting the cast and director and particularly in guiding the postproduction process.

The tasks of the drama and comedy executives diverge at the point of production. Since most comedies are shot on tape and drama projects are shot on film, there is little need for a drama executive to be on the set, except to greet the cast. Film is never shot in sequence, and normally only five to seven pages of television script are completed each day. It can take eight to twelve days to film a one-hour pilot and twenty-three or twenty-four days for a two-hour project.

During the production phase, the vice president of drama development views the *dailies* (the film shot the previous day) with producers and editors. They discuss wardrobe and makeup, the performances, and the different photographic angles used for each scene. If there are problems, the director is contacted on the set, and retakes are requested.

After shooting is complete, the director and producer work with the editors to assemble the finished picture. A rough cut of the film is screened for drama development executives, who suggest changes. If there are serious problems, a second or third screening of the revised rough cut might be necessary. When all parties are satisfied, postproduction people take control. When the film is in its final form, it is delivered to the network hierarchy and the audience testing department for screening.

Under the supervision of the vice president of drama development, forty to fifty scripts are developed for the network each season. Of these, only ten to twelve pilots are committed to production. NBC traditionally has favored two-hour pilots, believing that this affords the creative team time to develop the characters and tell a compelling story. There is also an economic factor involved. Two-hour pilots can be scheduled as movies, so even rejected pilots earn back some of their cost of production. CBS has a different philosophy about the length of dramatic pilots, preferring one-hour shows. CBS executives feel that one-hour pilots are more indicative of the actual series. ABC has a mixed approach, producing some one-hour pilots, many ninety-minute pilots, and a few two-hour pilots. They generally prefer the shorter form, feeling that two-hour projects tend to be easily padded. They can broadcast two rejected ninety-minute pilots as a special event and recoup some of their costs. Like NBC, they schedule rejected two-hour pilots as movies.

Throughout most of the year, the vice president of drama development and his or her counterpart in comedy function as buyers in the programming marketplace. During the spring, however, their roles are reversed, as they become sellers. Development executives must sell their pilots to their bosses and to the senior management of the network. The heads of drama and comedy suddenly find themselves in direct competition for valued spots in the fall schedule.

Current Drama Programs

As in current comedy programs, this area is vital to the well-being of the network. The current drama executive works with a contingent of subordinates to define and enhance scheduling strategies and bolster series weaknesses. It is a time-consuming job. Management must read and evaluate each script for every dramatic series on the network, suggest solutions to inherent problems, and view rough cuts of each episode before completion.

Current drama responsibilities include light action-adventure series with large quotients of humor (such as _The A-Team_) and more introspective character drama (such as _Cagney & Lacey_). In addition, current drama management analyzes the time slots, target audience, overall promotion, and possible new directions for every dramatic series on the network.

Current programming executives work closely with market research experts to analyze the strength of the series, the appropriateness of episodes for target audiences, and the competitive strength of each episode in the time slot. As a counterprogramming strategy, certain types of stories might be preferred over others.

After reviewing market research, the head of current programming meets with the production team, brainstorming new directions for the series. Before the fall premiere of a returning series, a game plan often is established for the entire season. Perhaps it involves the introduction of a new character, the elimination of an old character, a major change in one of the lead characters, a new direction for story ideas, a move to a new location, or any combination of the above.

Finally, the program executive tries to tailor episodes according to time slot information and demographic appeal. The staff tries to maximize audience appeal and to outdraw the competition. Aware of the different audiences for each time period, executives help tailor the themes and specific program elements for these audiences. For that reason, networks are more likely to cater to children and teenagers with humor, action, and machines which can become toys, like the Knight Rider car, at 8:00 P.M., while they would direct a 10:00 P.M. series more toward adults.

Miniseries

The most prestigious component of a network's program schedule is its miniseries. These mammoth projects require huge commitments of talent and dollars, and unlike all other forms of programming, they are planned years in advance. The position of vice president of miniseries is therefore usually awarded to a network programmer with considerable experience.

With only a few projects in development at any given time, the staff of the miniseries department is relatively small. While the origin of miniseries projects follows the same procedure as other network projects, the miniseries executives stay very close to these undertakings from inception to broadcast.

Planning is the key criterion for a project that can cost more than ten million dollars and might take a year or more to film. When a network initiates production of a miniseries, it has almost always targeted an important airdate. Advertising and publicity departments are alerted, and campaigns are designed and implemented while filming is still in progress.*

Miniseries began with large-scale dramas such as "QB VII" and "Rich Man, Poor Man." Eventually, the form evolved into shorter, sensational stories based on books, such as "Murder in Texas." More recently, miniseries (such as "Lace") have moved toward stylish, sexually oriented material. In most cases, the projects come from popular novels, including "Winds of War," "Centennial," and "The Thorn Birds."

The fact remains that, while prestigious, miniseries are not profitable. The networks have learned that very few miniseries can be repeated successfully, and then only after having rested for a year or more. The economics of primetime television normally demand that a show be played twice to return a profit to the network.

Similarly, the studio or production company producing the miniseries rarely breaks even. The production entity is banking on successful subsequent syndication or foreign release to make a profit. Many of the major studios, such as Universal, Warner Brothers, and 20th Century Fox, feel the financial outlay and risk are too great for the potential return. Consequently, most miniseries are produced by independent production companies such as David Wolper, Stonehenge Productions, and Aaron Spelling Productions.

Network executives often use miniseries as loss leaders. Although the projects are usually too expensive to recover the huge production costs from advertising revenue, if the miniseries is successful, it will garner high ratings and very large audiences. The network can schedule these important events during the crucial Nielsen ratings periods in November, February, and May. With stronger ratings, the network can increase the average audience base upon which they determine rates charged to advertisers.

Television Movies

Another executive is in charge of made-for-television movies. At one time, television movies were so successful that they merited their own

---

*For examples of these promotional campaigns, see Chapter 8.

time period. As they began to proliferate, however, movies competed against each other, and overexposure was inevitable. The series concept was abandoned, and the networks significantly reduced the number of original television films.

More recently, with the emergence of cable and videocassettes, the ratings value of theatrical motion pictures has diminished considerably, while production costs have escalated. Network executives are not interested in spending millions of dollars to broadcast the network premiere of a major motion picture that has already received national exposure on pay television and home video. As a consequence, they have again begun to focus on original made-for-television movies.

In the early stages, the process of developing movies is the same as that for other primetime shows. Movie executives listen to pitches (verbal presentations of concepts) from writers and producers. The network executive selects projects that are most likely to meet their needs. Demographics often play an important part in the decision-making process. For example, CBS looks for action-adventure films for its Saturday night lineup; NBC wants films with strong woman appeal to compete with *ABC Monday Night Football*.

From the standpoint of network programming, there is little, if any, residual value to television movies. They are shown only once before disappearing to syndication or postmidnight programming for insomniacs. Moreover, word-of-mouth, a valuable ingredient for any series to build a large audience, is useless with television movies. One friend might tell another about the terrific film on television last night, but that movie might not be repeated until months later.

What, then, is the purchase criteria for new television films? The executive seeks projects that can attract a very large audience and thus build the Nielsen ratings. Many television executives ask for a movie concept to be explained in one sentence, feeling that if the premise can be summarized effectively, it can be promoted to attract a wide audience. Most concepts for a highly promotable movie either exploit a popular contemporary issue (child abuse, AIDS, the convoluted legal system) or can be explained in a sentence beginning "What would happen if..." Think of some memorable television films, and you will recognize the succinct premises: "Brian's Song," "Something About Amelia," "The Day After," and "World War III."

Movie executives like concepts that are intriguing and attention-grabbing. At various times, all three networks employed market research firms to measure the intrinsic appeal of new concepts (an approach that has met with mixed success). In other cases, networks have developed advertising campaigns for television movies before production even began to ascertain the effectiveness of the concept.

In addition to appealing concepts, the movie excutive seeks projects that have widely known actors in leading roles. Many stars who normally shy away from television will perform in a prestigious television film. That, of course, enhances the prospects of promotion. Unfortunately, it also escalates the production budget.

In short, the essential function of network executives in charge of movies made for television is to balance a viable concept with suitable casting to maximize the viewing audience. Once a project has been selected and cast, however, the work of the movie department differs from that of its counterparts. While movie executives might watch dailies and supervise production, doing so is not as vital as it is for a series. Unless the movie is truly awful, the viewing audience is not likely to tune out. Too many bad movies in succession can frustrate the audience, but people who prefer to watch movies will tolerate an occasional clinker in the network schedule.

Network Production

Each network has its own production entity: ABC Circle Films, CBS Films, and NBC Productions. The chief executive is in charge of productions paid for and produced by the network itself. With a staff of writers, producers, and production supervisors, this division is responsible for the development and production of new programming for the network. This network operation is in direct competition with outside production companies, including the major studios.

The difference between network production divisions and independent companies is that the former can sell only to their own network. Even though there can be no favoritism in development decisions, the head of this division knows the network is eager to expand its own production activity and that this division can become an increasingly more important facet of network operations.

In the 1950s and 1960s, the networks owned or had ownership percentages in many of the shows they placed on the air, and they had production companies to produce these shows. One network, CBS, even bought its own studio, CBS Studio Center, in North Hollywood. After extensive hearings, the U.S. Justice Department decreed that in-house production organizations represented a conflict of interest. New Federal Communications Commission (FCC) rules were established limiting network financial participation to only two series at a given time.

As a consequence, network production companies were largely abandoned. Some diverted their attention to producing theatrical motion pictures or television movies. Only one network, NBC, maintained any regular series production with *Bonanza* and subsequently *Little House on the Prairie*.

More recently, the networks have successfully pleaded for a withdrawal of this production limitation, citing the increased competition from videocassettes, pay television, and cable. While there has been opposition from production companies and studios, the restrictions have been relaxed, and the networks are revitalizing their production divisions. The vice president in charge of network production, therefore, presides over a growing enterprise. In 1986 CBS produced *The Twilight Zone*, ABC produced *Moonlighting*, and NBC produced *Punky Brewster* and *Highway to Heaven*.

Specials

The executive in charge of specials usually works alone or with one or two assistants. This individual's responsibilities include occasional variety specials and special dramatic programs that fall outside the purview of the movie or miniseries department. This department is all that remains of a once-popular form, the variety show. At one time each network had a sizable department devoted exclusively to the development and production of variety programs. As such series declined in popularity, however, the need for a separate division decreased.

In many instances, dramatic specials have been produced outside the network, either by an advertiser or some other institution. Often these specials are packages put together with a major sponsor (such as AT&T or IBM) for special placement. The most famous of these is the *Hallmark Hall of Fame*. Hallmark produces these specials through its advertising agency and places them on the air just prior to greeting card events such as Christmas, Valentine's Day, and Mother's Day.

The vice-presidency of specials is considered by some to be a coveted position because of the quality of shows produced and because these expensive productions are filmed in exotic locations. Others at the network view the position as a dead end because development activity is relatively confined. The position usually is awarded to an experienced executive who no longer wishes to deal with the frantic pace and pressure of series programming.

Daytime Programs

While the attention of the media and the general public remains focused on primetime, network management recognizes that daytime is the breadbasket of network programming. With low-cost programs and more advertising time than primetime, daytime is a crucial economic contributor to network revenues. Since informational programming such as the *Today* show falls under the purview of the networks' news operations, the vice president of daytime programs is almost exclusively concerned with two entertainment forms, the game show and the soap opera.

Game Shows

In primetime the development process is geared for three seasons—fall, midseason, and spring. In contrast, the development of daytime programs is an ongoing process. Premieres can occur at any time of the year. The vice president of daytime programs and his or her subordinates are always available to listen to proposals for new game show ideas. The staff might want to develop and stockpile new game shows for future use: to initiate production immediately to bolster a sagging lineup or replace a weak or failing program.

One of the key functions of the head of daytime programming is the development of new game shows, which are classified as either hard games or soft games. *Hard games* are dependent on the game itself to sustain the momentum of the show. Players are chosen because of their knowledge and ability. The home viewer usually plays along, trying to answer the questions before the contestant. Some classic examples of the hard game are *The Price Is Right, Name That Tune,* and *Jeopardy.* In contrast, *soft games* are more concerned with humor and entertainment value. Usually these programs feature celebrity panelists. Most viewers do not realize that these shows are heavily scripted; the seemingly spontaneous ad-libs, jokes, and double entendres are prepared in advance by staff writers. Some classic examples of this form are *Hollywood Squares* and Groucho Marx's *You Bet Your Life.*

The development process for both hard and soft games is similar, beginning with the logic of the game itself. Developers of new concepts offer presentations, much the same way primetime developers present series concepts. Often, however, this involves graphs, charts, sample games, or even demonstration tapes, particularly if the show is complicated. The game show developer must demonstrate that the game is workable under all conditions. Once this has been established, other elements are considered, including attention to set design and types of prizes. When extravagant prizes become predominant, the shows sometimes are called *greed games.* In other shows, the fun of playing the game is the prime attraction.

The vice president of daytime oversees all phases of a new show, including the taping of a pilot episode. The final result is screened for network management and tested with different audiences. Once the show is on the air, it requires little network management. A well-staffed production unit can maintain the program for many years.

Soap Operas

The soap opera has been an intrinsic part of network daytime programming since the heyday of radio. It earned the nickname *soap opera* because it was originally produced and sponsored by soap manufacturers. While this is no longer true, the name has stuck, and the format has become a mainstay of daytime scheduling.

The vice president of daytime programs handles the development and production of daytime drama. Since the soap opera is a continuing drama, the major plot lines must be conceived and planned well in advance of production. Moreover, experience has shown that soap operas grow slowly. A network must be prepared to suffer intitial low ratings in the hope that the show eventually will catch the interest of daytime viewers. Network executives must be willing to wait a year, sometimes two, before a proper evaluation can be made concerning the success or failure of the show.

Before new shows are developed, the head of daytime programs evaluates the network's current schedule and ratings performance. If an older soap is failing and repeated attempts to revive the show are unsuccessful, a new daytime drama might be the answer. Similarly, if a scheduling opportunity presents itself, a new soap offering a competitive edge might get the go-ahead.

The development of new daytime dramas begins with production companies that have proven track records in this format. Soap operas are very specialized, and established players know the field. Generally, new concepts are presented in a form called a bible, a detailed plot line for the series that is written and developed by the head writer(s). All the continuing characters are profiled in detail, as are some of the significant story developments for the series. The vice president of daytime programs carefully evaluates the show bible, requesting changes and revisions until everyone is satisfied. Only then does he or she give the commitment to proceed.

Children's Programs

Program content is a major concern for the vice president of children's programs and his or her associates. Each network has a contingent of psychologists and sociologists who evaluate all the material. Programming for children has been the subject of intense scrutiny in recent years, both by congressional and legislative panels and by lobby groups such as Action for Children's Television (ACT). As a result, story content and characterizations in every Saturday morning show are monitored carefully. Both the creative people who develop and produce the programming and the network executives who supervise it must be cognizant of what is acceptable and what is not.

The head of children's programs supervises two areas of activity— Saturday morning programs and occasional weekday specials. While the specials offer the opportunity to try different types of quality shows, the central concern of the department is Saturday morning programming. There are some major differences between development of Saturday morning programming and that for other time periods. First, with rare exceptions, all Saturday morning shows are animated cartoons. Second, because of the expense of producing such programming, the number of episodes produced in any season (usually eighteen) is less than that for primetime, and cartoon segments usually are repeated six or more times.

Since animation is a time-consuming process, the Saturday morning development cycle is different from that for other dayparts. Daytime executives usually commit to new shows in February, and production begins shortly after. Due to the animation form and costs, no pilot is required. New show ideas are presented in storyboard form, with drawings and visual presentations.

It is interesting to note that some prominent network executives once served as head of children's programs, including Fred Silverman and Bud Grant, the current head of CBS.

CAREER TRAINING FOR NETWORK PROGRAMMERS

The people who are involved in network programming have a diverse background. Some come from production positions, others from research backgrounds, and still others from management training programs. There are no prerequisites for a management position, although some related work experience seems helpful. Among the more relevant resources are production assistants and gophers, legal and business school graduates, agents, researchers, writers, broadcast standards executives, management training graduates, and producers.

Assistants and Gophers

A number of network programming executives gained access to the industry either through employment as a personal assistant to a producer or as a gopher in a television production company. An assistant to a producer handles all the clerical and administrative chores, from typing and file maintenance to scheduling production meetings. A gopher is someone who is told to "go for" anything needed by the production crew, including coffee and doughnuts.

It is not at all unusual for bright, college-trained people to start their careers in these entry-level positions, which entail taking care of paper-work, running errands, arranging appointments, and serving coffee. With no formal training in television, the best learning experience is working inside an established operation, meeting people, making con-tacts, and seeing the intricate process of production. There usually is an unspoken agreement between the overqualified gopher (often with a graduate degree) and the employer that gives the young person access to the inner workings of the operation in exchange for low pay and the performance of sometimes menial tasks.

Legal and Business Majors

While less prevalent recently, in the past it was quite common for programming executives to have a background in law or business. One of the lesser known but important functions of program management is in the business affairs department of networks and studios. Individuals in this department negotiate everything from the amount of money paid guest stars to the complex terms and conditions of contracts for produc-ers, directors, and writers of pilots and series. They are fully aware of the terms of employment of everyone on staff and on particular productions, including option dates (for continued employment), credit requirements, royalties and residuals due, and unusual perks (a limou-sine, an air-conditioned motor home, an office with a view, a new car, and the like).

Since business executives work closely at all times with program-ming people, it is not unusual to find them occasionally crossing over to become programmers themselves. A number of prominent studio and television programming executives began their careers working in the business or legal department.

Former Agents

Agents interact at every level with network and production executives while representing major clients (writers, producers, directors, and ac-tors). With such a broad range of contacts, it is not unusual for an individual with an interest in programming to shift careers.

A career change usually occurs at one of two stages. First, as a young, apprentice agent, the person might decide to secure a buyer's role rather than a seller's. Several large agencies, such as William Morris, International Creative Management (ICM), and Creative Artists Agency (CAA), offer training programs for recent college graduates interested in the field. After a year or two working within the agency, these people develop contacts at the network, and a switch to network management is an option. The training they receive makes them credible additions to a network programming department.

The second opportunity seems to present itself after a successful career as an agent or packager at a much higher level. A number of television studio heads and key broadcast executives are former agents who made midcareer switches. These executives include Herman Rush, president of Columbia Pictures Television, and Harris Kattleman, president of 20th Century Fox-TV.

Researchers

While often derided as numbers men, computer jockeys, and the epitome of network interference, research departments have become an effective training ground for many highly placed program executives. Constant analysis of the viewing public and testing of new and existing television shows, coupled with access to all levels of network management, have proved to be an effective combination. For those interested in programming, the shift from researcher to programmer has become a well-worn path. Former researchers include Fred Pierce, former president of ABC entertainment; Harvey Shephard, vice-president of programming at CBS; Grant Rosenberg, vice president of Disney Television; and both authors of this text.

Writers

On occasion, script writers have traded in their word processors for a desk at a studio or network programming department. In most instances, however, these people were using writing as an entrée into programming. Most writers seem to prefer to stay on the creative side of the fence.

There are two reasons why writing is not a common path to network programming. First, the demand for superior writing ability is so great that the rise of a prolific and talented writer is meteoric. For example, one young man in his early twenties, Frank Lupo, went from driving a New York taxicab to executive producer at Steven Cannell Productions in less than five years. His story is not unique.

Second, the monetary rewards for writing success are commensurate with the writer's ability, and most successful writers are not eager to trade in their lucrative careers for a network job. Those writers who do become executives usually realize that their writing talents are competent at best. Still, they might be quite adept at critiquing stories and scripts and working with other writers. The need for good script doctors in both studio and network programming departments is great, and such writers willing to work as executives are always in demand.

Broadcast Standards Executives

Sharing the black hat of researchers are those persons designated as guardians of public taste. Work in the broadcast standards departments of the three networks is tedious, difficult, and unappreciated by the creative side of the business. The rules governing standards often seem arbitrary, and the standards executives are targets of derision.

The work, however, provides an excellent training ground for future programming executives. Broadcast standards workers must read every script thoroughly and view every film and tape before it is broadcast. They interact with writers and producers, network personnel, and studio executives. If they demonstrate flexibility, creativity, and an understanding of programming, it is relatively easy to exchange a censor's hat for that of programmer.

Management Training Program Graduates

The networks have instituted and operated their own management training programs at various times in the past. Usually managed through their New York offices, these on-again/off-again programs have enlisted top graduates from prestigious schools and given them the inside track to a network career. Successful graduates of such programs include Jeff Sagansky, former vice president of programs for NBC and current president of production at Tri-Star Pictures, and Ted Harbardt, vice president of movies made for television at ABC Entertainment.

Experienced Producers

Until this decade, the biggest source of network programmers was the pool of older, established independent producers who traded the uncertainty and pressure of active production for the security and more leisurely pace of a network office. This transition is now a rarity, since networks have turned more to younger producers, feeling that they are less rigid and more adventurous. Increased competition between networks and the competitive intrusion of cable, pay television, and home video have demanded increased flexibility and a heightened search for new program forms, making younger producers more attractive.

There is another reason why established producers tend to be outside network management. Network salaries simply cannot compete with those of independent creative people. Even a second-string producer or writer can earn two to three times the annual salary of a network program executive. The writer and producer of a renewable series are almost certainly millionaires.

The Network as a Training Ground

It is indeed ironic that program executives are thrust into the role of criticizing, modifying, accepting, and rejecting the work of more experienced and far better paid writers and producers. Because of this situation, many program executives feel that their current positions are only temporary. They view their work in programming as a stepping-stone to becoming an independent producer or the head of a production company.

The transition is reasonable, since an intimate understanding of network operations can be an enormous advantage to a producer and is essential for any studio production position. Many network executives have graduated to positions of prominence in the industry. Among the notables are Harve Bennett, who went from ABC to producing numerous series and the Star Trek movies; Esther Shapiro, who graduated from ABC to creating *Dynasty*; Dick Ebersol, who moved from NBC to *Saturday Night Live*; Len Hill, who worked at both NBC and ABC before forming his own production company; Charles Fries, Grant Tinker, Tom Werner, and Marcy Carsey, all of whom have had a significant impact on American primetime production and programming.

The Sellers of Primetime Television Programming

4

Now that we have looked at the functions of management at the network level, let's turn to the sellers and see how they function in the primetime marketplace. Most ideas are brought to the network for consideration by three primary industry resources: independent producers or production companies, major studios, and agents or packagers.

INDEPENDENT PRODUCERS AND PRODUCTION COMPANIES

Independent producers run the gamut from one person who holds an option on a creative work to one who heads a production company with several network shows on the air. Their goal is multifaceted: find new projects, hire the best people to develop them, sell the concepts to the network, produce them brilliantly, get the shows on the air in a perfect time slot, keep the shows on the air for several years, and develop more concepts while supervising a successful long-running series.

A producer might come up with his or her own idea or might be interested in concepts pitched by writers or other producers. Those ideas can be based on headlines in the newspaper, popular song lyrics, or an old paperback in the attic. It does not matter where the idea comes from; it does matter how the concept is fleshed out and presented to the network.

As discussed earlier, the producer is the key person in charge of all the creative elements for a network show. He or she oversees every aspect of series development, packaging, and production. Even acquisition of rights lies within the producer's domain. If a project is based on a book or short story, rights must be cleared before development can begin. The producer then oversees the entire adaptation process, from creative supervision of the script through packaging and selling.*

Independent producers might be headquartered on the lot of a major studio, either leasing their own office suite or working under a staff contract with the studio. In the latter situation, they might be hired by the studio to produce ongoing series or develop new ones. Under this contract, the producer is a partner in the programs he or she creates and must bring them to the studio for first refusal.

Established producers who have a strong track record form their own companies. These companies might seem small when compared to studio operations, but financial gains can be exceptional. Overhead is low and profits derived from sales can be returned to the development coffers. Some production companies have met with outstanding success in developing and selling network products. Among them are Embassy Communications, MTM Enterprises, Aaron Spelling Productions, Stephen Cannell Productions, and Charles Fries Productions.

Embassy Communications

Norman Lear and his partners have been responsible for developing some of the most important television comedy programs. Stressing social themes as the base of character conflicts, they introduced prime-time viewers to some of the best-loved characters in series such as *All in the Family, Sanford and Son,* and *Maude.* While much of primetime comedy centers on situations and fantasies, these shows introduced characters who dealt with racial bigotry, abortion, breast cancer, and other powerful themes. Audiences reacted warmly to these characters, generating enough enthusiasm for spin-off series.

Over the years, Norman Lear has worked closely with various partners to develop projects through different production companies, including TAT, Tandem, and Embassy. His early partner, Bud Yorkin, helped bring *All in the Family* to television. Later partners, Jerry Perenchio and Al Burton, helped manage Embassy and supervised the development of quality network comedy series such as *Silver Spoons, The Facts of Life, Diff'rent Strokes, Who's the Boss?,* and *227.*

_____
*For more on producing, see Horace Newcomb and Robert Alley, *The Producer's Medium: Conversations with Creators of American TV* (New York: Oxford University Press, 1983).

In addition to half-hour situation comedies, Embassy has expanded into made-for-television movies, with mixed success. The company has produced well-received projects such as "Heartsounds," "Grace Kelly," and "Eleanor, The First Lady." But they also produced "Generation," an ABC movie that ranked at the bottom of all made-for-television films in 1985.

Nothing in the television industry remains static, and the prospect of business mergers, new successes, and sudden failures always looms ahead. As a result of their programming dominance in comedy and their escalating financial stature, Embassy Communciations was acquired in 1985 by the Coca Cola Company. The new company has retained a strong commitment to new programming.

MTM Enterprises

Mary Tyler Moore is the recognizable entity behind MTM, but other executives have helped the company maintain its prominent place in the market. In the early years, Grant Tinker was a prime mover for the company, helping develop some outstanding comedy shows with interesting characters and environments. These included *The Mary Tyler Moore Show, Rhoda,* and *Taxi.* His ability to develop tasteful and appealing shows and to get along with producers and network buyers led to an unusual situation: Grant Tinker was offered a top network position. After great deliberation, he finally jumped the fence to become a network buyer.

Interestingly, MTM has since earned a reputation for developing and producing high-quality drama series. MTM producer Steven Bochco developed and supervised *Hill Street Blues*, while others at MTM have developed and sold one-hour projects such as *Remington Steel* (Michael Gleason) and *St. Elsewhere* (Bruce Paltrow).

Some producers stay with a studio or a production company for a long time in a successful partnership, while others move on to different studios depending on network programming sales. Dan Wilcox, who produced the last six years of *M*A*S*H* at 20th Century Fox, moved to MTM, where he produced *Newhart* and later supervised development for the company.

Just prior to working on *Newhart*, he worked with Steven Bochco on a short-lived series about an amateur baseball team (*Bay City Blues*). Bochco's concept featured a group of young men as diverse as the characters on *Hill Street Blues* who had a passion for playing amateur baseball.

A meeting was set up with the networks to pitch the idea. Bochco had his secretary buy a new baseball, which he promptly tossed around to the executives in the meeting. The network was unsure about the concept, not quite convinced that it would have enough interest for general audiences. Bochco assured them that playing ball was a universal dream, connecting most men (and some women) to early childhood dreams. He told them to look at their own behavior in the meeting. Here they were, grown men, tossing around the ball as if they were alumni from the same high school. The producer contended that most American males have that secret child inside, and that's what would make this series great. The deal was made. Unfortunately, the series never had a clear focus or an identifiable group of characters, and it folded in one season.

After some internal conflicts over the direction of *Hill Street Blues*, Bochco left MTM and independently developed the very successful and upscale dramatic series, *L.A. Law*. Back at the MTM lot, Dan Wilcox served as executive producer of *Newhart*, providing new blood to a comedy series that was fumbling in the ratings. His personable style as a producer came through in the series, and it was picked up for a new season.

Given the track record of MTM Enterprises and its ability to draw top producing talent, the company will remain a major supplier of primetime programming for the networks.

Aaron Spelling Productions

Aaron Spelling has had an exclusive production contract with ABC for many years. He is a master of escapist fare, having created some widely appealing shows. In association with Doug Cramer, he developed and sold *The Love Boat*, and both served as executive producers of the series. Earlier he teamed up with Len Goldberg on a number of quick series sales, including *The Mod Squad*.

More recently, Spelling has moved into the primetime soap opera sphere, producing *Hotel* with Doug Cramer and *Dynasty* with Doug Cramer and Richard and Esther Shapiro. In an effort to capture some of the contemporary audience attracted by shows such as *Miami Vice* (produced by Universal TV), he created and sold a short-lived series called *Hollywood Beat*, again in association with Doug Cramer.

Spelling also has been active in developing movies of the week. He created the television pilot film for *MacGruder & Loud*, which did well in the ratings. His multipart film "Hollywood Wives" drew some of the highest ratings of any television film in the 1985 season. *Finder of Lost Loves* served admirably as a pilot, and other television films produced by Spelling performed well in the Nielsen ratings. Among them are "Glitter" and "Shooting Stars."

Stephen Cannell Productions

After a successful career at Universal Studios, where he worked on a number of primetime series and was one of the individuals responsible for *The Rockford Files*, Steve Cannell left the confines of a major studio to open his own production company. After a few unsuccessful attempts, he created *The Greatest American Hero*, followed by a run of prominent series such as *The A-Team*, *Hardcastle and McCormick*, *Riptide*, and *Hunter*. *The A-Team* was initiated in-house by NBC and offered to Cannell to develop. It became a long-term success for the network.

Steve Cannell remains a strong supplier of primetime series to the networks, with particular emphasis on action formats.

Charles Fries Productions

Charles Fries Productions is responsible for some of television's most memorable dramatic television films and miniseries. At one time Fries was head of production for Screen Gems, Columbia Picture-TV's comedy factory that produced series such as *I Dream of Jeannie*, *Bewitched*, *The Partridge Family*, *The Flying Nun*, and *The Monkees*. Later he moved to Metromedia Producers Corporation (MPC), where he was in charge of all new projects developed for the networks, including television films.

Fries then formed his own production company, inviting independents to submit projects for consideration as joint ventures. His company developed and produced a wide range of successful primetime television movies and miniseries. Among them are "The Martian Chronicles," "Flight of 401," and "Samaritan." His company retains a prominent financial and creative position in the production of television films.

Other Production Companies

Some of television's most appealing shows come from a variety of sources outside the major production entities. Established producers such as Alan Landsburg, Stan Shpetner, Dick Berg, Len Hill, Renee Valente, and David Wolper develop and supervise a great number of successful primetime series and films. Similarly, companies such as Orion Television, New World Television, Tri-Star, Viacom and Centerpoint usually are represented in primetime programming.

Independent producers also can have considerable clout. One example is when Marcy Carsey and Tom Werner joined forces with Bill Cosby to create *The Cosby Show*, one of the network's runaway hits of the 1985 television season.

These production companies and independent producers, along with many others, have made a significant mark on primetime television. They are prominent sellers, competing head-on with major studios for the few network primetime slots.

Development Activity in Production Companies

In each production company, one person usually is designated head of development. A typical staffing situation might have one person in charge of all new programs, with one or two assistants. They meet daily with writers, producers, agents, and network executives to come up with the best concepts for potential network sales.

The development staff responds to submissions that come in from all sources, and if they are interested in a concept, they will propose a deal through their business affairs department. The deals are fairly standard, offering an option for the right to sell the project to the networks. This usually involves a small amount of money paid up front to the creator, with higher fees and services payable at the time a network commits to pilot development or production.

Producers know that selling primetime programming is a risky business. Chances of getting new shows on the air are slim, yet hope springs eternal for buyers and sellers. Networks commit to more projects than they can possibly use, and they keep hordes of reserves on the shelf. Few projects get to pilot production, and even fewer get aired. Despite the staggering odds of a new series surviving the season, the primary objective for production companies remains the same—series longevity. If a show can earn high enough ratings in its time slot, along with audience loyalty, the prospects are enhanced for achieving the company's ultimate goal—network time slot dominance—and the final reward—a lucrative future in syndication.

MAJOR STUDIOS

For many years, major studios have been the unheralded champions of film and television production. This was not always the case, however.

In fact, they initially wanted to produce exclusively for the motion picture box office. In the fifties and early sixties, major studios competed with each other for motion picture audiences, gambling hundreds of millions of dollars on film spectacles that failed at the box office. As a direct consequence, they were forced to reexamine their positions in the industry.

Motion picture studios first recognized the financial opportunities offered by television in the mid-fifties, when they permitted television to purchase more than twenty-five hundred films produced before 1948. In a subsequent move to gain a foothold, they created their television divisions to produce and distribute television shows. They also rented their production facilities to independent producers, opened up their studios as tourist attractions, and sold their back lots to real estate developers. Many were taken over by entertainment conglomerates.*

The studios realized at a critical juncture that television represented a profitable venture and the relationship between the studios and television has become symbiotic.

Major studios are at a distinct advantage when it comes to resources available for television program development and production. Every corporate and departmental resource can be tapped for developing, producing, and selling television and film projects. The resources are vast and sophisticated, but the costs of sustaining those resources are high. Administrative overhead is enormous, and profits from network sales often are disbursed to keep the studio overhead in line. The overhead includes production failures and overruns, payroll for hundreds of union employees, and upkeep of state-of-the-art film and video facilities.

As mentioned before, each studio has a television division with its own programming identity. Studios vie for the most gifted writers and producers, some of whom move from studio to studio. Others stay at one studio for years. Producers who head hit shows and develop and sell new projects are worth their weight in gold for major studios such as Universal Studios, Columbia Pictures-TV, Paramount, Warner Brothers, 20th Century Fox, MGM/UA, Lorimar-Telepictures, and Walt Disney.

Let's look at each studio, then examine the structure of a typical television division.**

---

*See Thomas Bohn and Richard Stromgren, _Light and Shadows: A History of Motion Pictures_ (New York: Alfred Publishing, 1975), 396–98, 411–13.

**Early historical profiles of the studios are discussed in Bohn and Stromgren, _Light and Shadows: A History of Motion Pictures_, 235–56; see also Douglas Gomery, _The Hollywood Studio System_ (New York: St. Martin's Press, 1986). For a classic history of motion picture studios, also see Arthur Knight, _The Liveliest Art: A Panoramic History of the Movies_ (New York: Macmillan, 1957).

Universal Television

Universal Pictures is one of Hollywood's largest and oldest studios. It dates back to 1912, when it was a top silent-film company. In the 1920s Universal produced a great number of comedies, Westerns, and novelty features. The studio continued making B films when sound appeared, and throughout the thirties it became widely known for its entertaining B musicals and horror films. In the 1950s it was taken over by MCA, which divested itself of the talent agency business to devote all its management energies to production. As a result Universal has become the most prolific supplier of television programs.

Over the years, Universal-TV signed many renowned television producers. Those producers turned out an extraordinary number of new series, miniseries, and television films. In the 1985-86 season alone, Universal produced programs for every network, including shows such as *The Insiders, Airwolf, The Equalizer, George Burns Comedy Week, Magnum, P.I., Misfits of Science, Simon & Simon, Alfred Hitchcock Presents, Amazing Stories, Knight Rider, Miami Vice,* and *Murder, She Wrote.* They also produced many successful television films, including "Code of Vengeance" and "Kojack: The Belarus File."

Producers on the lot are largely responsible for coming up with new series and television films, as well as overseeing production of their shows. If a series is sold to the networks, the producer who supervised its development generally will serve as executive producer and might oversee other network projects.

Among the producers located on the Universal lot during the 1986 television season were Peter Fischer (*Murder, She Wrote*), Michael Mann and Anthony Yerkovich (*Miami Vice*), and Christopher Crowe (*Alfred Hitchcock Presents*). Sometimes producers wind up with offices at different studios—if they are working with those studios on network deals. For example, at Universal, Glen Larson created *Knight Rider* and initiated the project that became *Magnum, P.I.* (with executive producer Donald Bellisario writing and producing the pilot). He later moved to 20th Century Fox, where he produced *The Fall Guy.*

Universal-TV benefits from the creative track record of people under contract for both motion pictures and television. Steven Spielberg, the motion picture wunderkind, was headquartered on the lot and wanted to create a new television series. The one-half-hour show *Amazing Stories* was developed under the banner of his Amblin Productions in association with Universal. The studio believed that Spielberg's name alone could carry the weight of any new television series.

Spielberg's pitch for a new series was simple: Audiences had missed this kind of programming since the early days of the original *Twilight Zone* and *Alfred Hitchcock Presents* series (the latter of which was updated by Universal for the same television season). Moreover, the anthology format allowed Spielberg to draw on top Hollywood stars who ordinarily would not have the time or interest in doing a television series. Exceptional actors, directors, and writers could join the project, as they would be working on a fast schedule. Given the executive producer and the inherent advantages of the package, Brandon Tartikoff, president of NBC entertainment, felt the network was taking a minor gamble.

Incidentally, this was not the first time suspense anthologies had made a network comeback. In the early seventies, NBC spoke with motion picture producer William Castle, who specialized in B-grade horror films and had produced the successful *Rosemary's Baby* for Columbia Pictures. In a luncheon meeting, Castle convinced NBC executives that a series based on *Rosemary's Baby* would draw an incredibly large and faithful audience. They agreed, but they wanted to see something on paper showing how the film could be adapted for television. After agonizing about the possibilities, Castle worked with a program executive at Columbia Pictures-TV to come up with a salable concept. They eventually decided to market a formula inherent in the film's story—identifiable people in recognizable places caught up in sudden extraordinary events. That became the basis of *Ghost Story*, the first new generation suspense anthology series. The series attracted some of Hollywood's finest talent, including Helen Hayes, Melvyn Douglas, Jason Robards, Mariette Hartley, Patty Duke Astin, Angie Dickinson, Martin Sheen, Janet Leigh, and Mike Farrell.

Columbia Pictures-TV

Columbia Pictures was founded in 1924 under the tenacious reign of Harry "King" Cohn and Jack Cohn. They had little money to compete with other studios for box office stars, relying instead on the capabilities of directors such as Frank Capra, Howard Hawks, Lewis Milestone, George Cukor, Leo McCarey, and George Stevens. Despite unprecedented offers of profit sharing, Columbia had difficulty holding on to directors because of Harry Cohn's autocratic and heavy-handed rule.

Ironically, it was Columbia Pictures that first established a television division, at a time when film stars were not allowed to appear on television. Studios had unsettling backlogs of films, box office attendance was slipping, production costs were climbing, and television was holding audiences captive in their living rooms. In an effort to take advantage of television, Columbia formed a subsidiary called Screen Gems in 1952 to produce commercials and programs for the networks.

Throughout the fifties and sixties, Screen Gems was known in the industry as a comedy factory, turning out an unending array of half-hour situation comedies, including *Bewitched, I Dream of Jeannie, The Partridge Family, The Flying Nun,* and many others. At various times, the studio was headed by Jackie Cooper, Charles Fries, and Len Goldberg. Some of the producers under contract included Harry Ackerman, Sidney Sheldon, and William Asher, who had multiple comedy series on the air.

In the early seventies, Columbia sold its Hollywood lot and moved to the Burbank Studios, which it shares with Warner Brothers. The company renamed its television division Columbia Pictures-TV and has been a prime supplier of comedy and drama programs ever since. In 1986, the Coca Cola Company purchased Columbia Pictures-TV, just as it had acquired Embassy Communications.

Producers at Columbia have been relatively successful throughout the 1980s, developing and selling series such as *Hell Town* (Robert Blake), *Crazy Like a Fox* (Jack Warden), and *Ripley's Believe It or Not* (in association with Ray Stark and Jack Haley, Jr.). Independent producers at the studio have been involved with dramatic television film projects, including the biographical saga "Robert Kennedy and His Times," and action-oriented television films such as "Deceptions," "Deadly Messages," and "Malibu."

Paramount

Paramount was one of the dominant studios during the silent-film era and historically has demonstrated a great respect for producers and directors. During the early days, Paramount signed directing luminaries such as Cecil B. DeMille, Ernst Lubitsch, and Josef von Sternberg. Although it could not compete with studios like MGM for stars, it did sign directors and attract some major performers (including Marlene Dietrich, Mae West, Gary Cooper, and Bob Hope) for studio films. During those days, Paramount turned out different styles of films, from light comedy to theatrical spectacles.

Throughout the years, Paramount has operated as a motion picture studio with cyclical periods of financial success, failure, and conglomerate mergers. The studio did not produce or distribute any films for television until 1953, when it established a formal ongoing relationship with ABC. Since that time, Paramount-TV has been a prime supplier of new programs for the networks.

Paramount produced some classic action series including *Mannix,* and acquired *Star Trek* and *Mission: Impossible* from the dissolved Lucille Ball, Desi Arnaz organization (Desilu). Many of their other shows were vintage comedies, such as *The Brady Bunch, The Odd Couple,* and

Love, American Style. The studio has sustained its interest in comedy with shows such as *Happy Days*, which generated viewer loyalty, syndication profits, and series spin-offs. *Cheers*, produced by Les Charles, Glen Charles, and James Burrows, along with *Taxi*, feature intriguing characters who have won the hearts of network viewers. Paramount producers also have created comedy series such as *Webster* (Bruce Johnson) and *Family Ties* (Gary David Goldberg).

Some independent producers on the Paramount lot are known for their dramatic projects. One of them, Dick Berg, owns his own company (Stonehenge), which produces dramatic television films in association with Paramount-TV. Berg was responsible for developing some of Paramount's more renowned successes in television drama, including the miniseries "Space," the multipart film "Wallenberg: A Hero's Story," and a short-lived one-hour dramatic series called *Hometown*.

Warner Brothers

In the thirties and forties, Warner Brothers was known as the "depression studio" because it produced films showing the realities of the Great Depression. Those projects took the form of gangster films, as well as Busby Berkely musicals. Warner Brothers signed some of the most popular male stars of the period, including Edward G. Robinson, James Cagney, Humphrey Bogart, George Arliss, Errol Flynn, and Paul Muni.

Throughout the forties and fifties, Warner Brothers remained in competition with the other studios, waging a bitter battle to win motion picture audiences. The studio had no interest in producing for television until the mid-fifties, when it began to realize that television program production could be a profitable venture.

In 1954 Warner Brothers signed an agreement with ABC to produce television projects, and not long after that it formed a television subsidiary called Seven Arts. That television production division was successful in producing a number of early television series and eventually became known as Warner Brothers TV.

Warner Brothers continues to be a major supplier of comedy and drama for primetime television. In the 1985 season, the studio sold several network series, including *Night Court*, *Spenser for Hire*, *Scarecrow and Mrs. King*, and *Growing Pains*.

20th Century Fox

20th Century Fox did not make a splash on the Hollywood scene until 1935, when Darryl F. Zanuck became vice president of production. At that time, the studio signed only a few stars to studio contracts. Shirley Temple graced the 20th Century Fox screen in her formidable years; Charlie Chan drew audiences to the mystery genre; Will Rogers, a major American talent, died a year after signing; Betty Grable was under contract during the late forties and early fifties.

Like other studios, 20th Century Fox was engaged in a battle to survive throughout the fifties and sixties. In the fifties, Hollywood feature production was cut in half, and throughout the sixties production costs climbed exorbitantly. Meanwhile, box office figures plummeted to new lows. In the midst of that financial crisis, the studio produced a multimillion dollar musical, *The Sound of Music* (1965). The film grossed more than $135 million at the box office, and every studio in town tried to capitalize on the perceived audience.

In a desperate attempt to repeat that success, studios invested millions of dollars in large-scale projects. 20th Century Fox committed untold millions for major spectacles such as *Dr. Doolittle, Star,* and *Tora! Tora! Tora!* (the latter film alone was budgeted at $25 million). At the same time, Paramount poured its resources into *Paint Your Wagon* ($20 million), *Darling Lili* ($19 million), and *The Molly Maguires* ($17 million). Despite the studios' efforts, the audiences remained at home, and the studios suffered devastating losses. By 1969, 20th Century Fox found itself with more than $300 million in inventory and more than $30 million in losses.

During this intense period, while studios were selling their back lots and merging with corporate entities, they came to realize that television helped them stay afloat. Their television subsidiaries were turning profits and keeping the studios on their feet.

20th Century Fox-TV has remained a strong supplier of television programs for the networks. In recent years, several dramatic projects have been developed by independent producers and in-house development executives. Don Brinkley supervised *Trapper John, M.D.* and Glen Larson developed *The Fall Guy.* On a more ambitious scale, producers John Furia and Barry Orringer adapted Ernest Hemingway's book *The Sun Also Rises* for television.

Comedy program development also remained strong. The most important 20th Century Fox project probably was *M*A*S*H,* which has won a place in the Smithsonian Institution as part of American popular culture. Other comedies developed more recently by 20th Century Fox's television division have not been able to match *M*A*S*H*'s success, but they have appeared on the network schedule.

An important corporate move took place in 1986 with the formation of Fox Broadcasting Company and its plans for a fourth entertainment network for independent stations. Fox bought several independent stations and signed deals with network affiliates nationwide in an effort to compete head-on with the networks. Earlier attempts by other sources to start a fourth network have failed, but advertisers seem particularly optimistic about Fox's programming strategy, which is targeted at young adults.

According to Marc Goldstein, senior vice president of Ogilvy & Mather, a major advertising agency, Fox's approach is refreshingly different from past attempts. Among these differences are that Fox is not asking for support before pilots are produced, programming concepts are targeted specifically at a young adult audience, and advertising prices promise to be lower than those at the existing networks. Another advertising executive, Bill Croasdale, senior vice president of the ad agency Batten, Barton, Durstine & Osborne (BBDO), has reinforced the view that Fox programming would be competitive: "We're looking at them as a true fourth network," he said.*

MGM/UA

In the 1930s, as heads of the illustrious Metro-Goldwyn-Mayer Studios, Louis B. Mayer and Irving Thalberg reigned supreme. Thalberg, who started his career as Carl Laemmle's secretary at Universal, joined MGM as vice president of production in 1924. Having great respect for the talents of producers, directors, and stars, Thalberg signed some of the top talent in Hollywood to studio contracts. In a short time, MGM became known as the "home of the stars." Legendary actors of the thirties and forties signed exclusive contracts, including John Barrymore, Jackie Cooper, Joan Crawford, Clark Gable, Spencer Tracy, Helen Hayes, and Greta Garbo.

MGM had no interest in television programming until the mid-fifties, when other studios recognized television as a serious buyer of film programs. While other studios formed and activated television subsidiaries, MGM-TV was formed to develop and produce projects for the networks. In the 1980s, MGM merged with United Artists Entertainment, and their television projects have been produced by MGM-TV in association with United Artists Entertainment (U/A-TV).

The studio has had mixed success in television, with a fairly good record of programming sales but never approaching the production sales of some of their competitors (most notably Universal). Some of the dramatic television films produced by MGM/UA have done very well in the ratings, however. Among them are "The Dirty Dozen: Next Mission" and "Paper Dolls." One of television's most respected dramatic producers, David Gerber, who produced *Police Story* (for

---

*"Fox Broadcasting Goes to Madison Avenue," *Broadcasting*, 9 June 1986, 41.

Columbia) and *Lady Blue*, among other series and television movies, took over creative control of the television division in 1985.

In 1986 Turner Broadcasting System (TBS) acquired MGM/UA for approximately $1.5 billion. Owner Ted Turner reportedly wanted to acquire the vast programming material available in the classic film library of MGM for his own "superstation" WTBS. In a quick turn-around, he sold the United Artists and MGM film production and distribution businesses back to Kirk Kerkorian, former MGM owner. Turner sold the MGM studio lot to Lorimar-Telepictures. *Variety* reported the business deal in these terms: "The breakup of MGM into its various parts signals the end of an era of one of the entertainment industry's most venerated studios, and also notes for the record book the briefest reign (74 days) of any film company mogul—TBS owner Ted Turner."*

Lorimar–Telepictures

Lorimar Productions and Telepictures Corporation merged in 1986, with Merv Adelson and Jay Solomon serving as chairmen of the board. The merger created a vast corporate entity capable of purchasing independent television stations and newspapers. As noted above, the company acquired MGM's studio lot from Turner Broadcasting System in 1986. The price: $190 million in cash.

Lorimar was founded in 1963 as a partnership between Lee Rich and Merv Adelson to develop television programs and theatrical films. Rich left the company in 1986 to become chairman of United Artists.

In the early years of development, Lorimar created shows such as *Eight Is Enough* and *The Waltons*, staples of family viewing. In 1978 it produced *Dallas*, which made television history as a primetime soap opera. That series has endured many years of character changes and interrelationships.

Lorimar has since cornered the market on primetime soap operas and miniseries. *Knots Landing* was a spin-off from *Dallas* and is produced by Michael Filerman and David Jacobs. *Falcon Crest* is another primetime soap opera, initially supervised by Earl Hamner and Michael Filerman. The company also has developed dramatic miniseries such as "Sybil," and "Blood and Orchids."

In just one television season (1985), Lorimar sold and produced some of the most successful movies of the week and miniseries. Among

---

*"Turner Keeps Pics, Drops Rest of MGM," *Variety*, 11 June 1986, 3.

them were "Christopher Columbus," "Lace," "Berrenger's," "Two of a Kind," "Wedding on Walton's Mountain," and "A Death in California." They also produced two comedy series, *Valerie* and *Perfect Strangers*.

Telepictures was founded in 1978 by Michael Solomon and Michael Garin. Their expertise—original programming for syndication—included animated children's shows (*Thundercats*) and programs such as *The People's Court* and *Love Connection*.

Walt Disney

Walt Disney Studios was founded on the incredible animation talents of Walt Disney and his executives, producers, and technical staff. The studio is primarily interested in providing family-oriented fare, and it produces major animation projects for motion pictures with unmatched success.

Walt Disney realized, however, that television represented a gold mine for projects developed at his studio, so he signed an exclusive agreement with ABC in the fifties. Disney Studios produced a weekly animated series for family audiences and eventually expanded into film comedy and drama. The company also produced a number of family-oriented films and science fiction movies, with mixed box office success.

As for television, after a corporate takeover in 1984, most of the old guard was replaced with experienced studio heads from Paramount (Michael Eisner and Jeff Katzenburg) and Warner Brothers (Frank Wells). As a result, the studio recently has expanded into new aspects of program production and has made distribution deals with independent producers. One of the first distribution deals was with Paul Witt, Tony Thomas, and Susan Harris (creators of *Soap*) for *The Golden Girls*, a comedy series focusing on the lives of four older women (Beatrice Arthur, Betty White, Rue McClanahan, and Estelle Getty). The series has been a major hit with national audiences and critics.

The Television Division of Major Studios

Within the major studios, the television division is responsible for developing, producing, and selling network shows. The management structure is generally the same as that at independent production companies and the networks. A divisional vice president oversees the various program departments, and each department has a director, a manager, and a small support staff.

Program Development

The staff meets regularly with writers and producers to identify potentially viable program concepts and to follow through on scripting, casting, and pilot production. The department head decides on which projects are worth pursuing, and the division staff receives advice and input from other departments, including legal, business affairs, production, and current programming.

Business Affairs

The business affairs department oversees negotiations between the studio and the networks, as well as negotiations between the studio and agents, producers, actors, directors, and other staff members. This office sends out reminders to studio executives about contracts that are coming due, credits required for specific productions, and other business matters relevant to a new or ongoing show.

Legal Affairs

The legal department works closely with business affairs, providing contractual backup for all deals. The staff alerts studio executives to potential litigation problems and closes deals on production contracts. The legal department also checks into any significant problems associated with a new show, including contracts, rights and clearances, and other relevant matters.

Production

Production is the heart of a studio's business, and the head of production often is in charge of the studio. This person works very closely with the head of program development and helps decide what will be produced, by whom, with what budget, and in what facilities. The production head meets regularly with production coordinators and division heads, approving all major expenses or commitments associated with new and ongoing productions.

Current Programming

The head of current programming oversees a staff of directors, managers, and support personnel to maintain the strength of every show produced by the studio. Some staff members specialize in a particular genre (drama, comedy, specials, television films), while others specialize in dealing with specific network projects.

Although the departmental configurations might differ from studio to studio, the general staffing responsibilities remain the same, as do the basic objectives: to keep each studio's shows on the network schedule for a minimum of three years.

AGENTS OR PACKAGERS

Agents, especially those promoting their own clients, often are involved in selling ideas and programs to the networks. A very large agency such as William Morris, International Creative Management, or Creative Artists Agency, represents clients in all fields of entertainment, including actors, directors, writers, and producers. A show that is creatively packaged by a large agency is a comparatively low risk for the networks, since the script has been developed, stars are committed to the project, and established producers will supervise the effort. The package is more expensive for the network, however, as the agency receives a packaging fee (which usually amounts to 15 percent of the purchase price) for its efforts.

The administration of a large agency is handled by vice presidents who oversee different divisions, including areas such as television, motion pictures, concerts (music and variety), legitimate stage (theater), and literary activities (books). Each department head oversees the daily activities of agents and junior agents (who are just learning the field) and has authority over the day-to-day operations of the division.

A typical day finds the ubiquitous agent on the phone with clients or buyers and in meetings with clients, network executives, producers, or studio executives. In addition, agents read and evaluate prospects for new material; follow up leads for new television or film offers; negotiate deals with the networks, studios, and independent production companies; and assuage damaged egos.

A good agent meets with clients to discuss submission strategies for new ideas, identifying the most appropriate network, studio, or independent production company. Internal staff meetings are held to discuss prospects for new concepts submitted by clients and the packaging potential of each project.

Packaging is the trademark of a large agency. It is meticulously done, involving top clients represented by the agency worldwide. There is also a downside to the process. Considering the exceptionally high price tag, the network looks very carefully at all elements of a package. If the buyer is uncomfortable with any element, the deal can be rejected. If a network executive feels uneasy about the costar or the director, for example, the project will never be produced.

Unlike corporate agencies that offer heavyweight packaging and global contacts, independent agencies represent a smaller number of clients with a specific expertise. Hollywood literary agents handle a select list of writers and producers, while smaller talent agents handle actors exclusively. In New York, independent literary agents generally represent novelists and playwrights, as most primetime television writers are on the West Coast.

Many independent agencies are surprisingly well staffed, with senior agents, junior agents, and clerical assistants. Some companies (such as Adams Ray & Rosenberg and Sy Fischer Company) have an impressive list of clients who are well established in the television industry. Since these companies represent writers, producers, and directors, they also can provide minipackaging services. New material written by one client can be submitted for consideration to a producer who also is a client. The process is simple and consistent with the idea of providing a marketable product to network buyers. Many of the smaller independent agencies in Hollywood have been responsible for selling some of primetime television's most enduring series, miniseries, and television films.

Developing Series for Primetime Television

Angela Lansbury stars as leading character Jessica Fletcher in the series
Murder, She Wrote. Here she is shown with costars Tom Bosley (left)
and Claude Akins (right).

5

Developing Series Concepts

This chapter focuses on the process through which the most basic idea is developed into an appealing series presentation for the network. It explores techniques and practices for creating the most professional and marketable television series proposal.

Many people think that a concept is the most important element in a television series. Every day, people write letters to networks offering their ideas for new series. Recently a network executive was chuckling over a letter he had received that day. It ended with the statement, "Please send your check to. . . ."

Television professionals recognize that concepts can be one of the least important elements in the development of a series. Everyone has ideas; it is the successful implementation of those ideas that counts.

CRITERIA FOR EFFECTIVE TELEVISION CONCEPTS

The logical question is "What makes a good concept for series development?" There are three criteria: the desirability of the idea; the ability to sustain the concept over many episodes; internal conflict among series characters.

The Desirability of the Idea

The first question usually asked of any new project is "Why will people watch this show?" In primetime programming, each series must attract a sufficient audience to survive. Network television demands very large audiences, numbering tens of millions, to achieve competitive ratings. New series must be inherently desirable and appealing to draw potential viewers.

Any idea for a series must demonstrate desirability. This means that a concept should answer at least one of the following questions.

1.   *Is the basic storytelling arena interesting?* Is the idea set in a desirable and exotic locale (Hawaii, San Francisco, the Caribbean)? Does it feature interesting occupations (deep-sea diver, astronaut, race-car driver)? Does it have the ability to use unusual and fascinating machinery or technology (special cars, weapons, high-tech equipment)? Does it lend itself to an interesting, visual approach?

2.   *Does the concept represent some form of wish fulfillment?* In our contemporary, technological society, there are few places people can turn to satisfy the frustrations of everyday life. Many long-running television series play on this frustration by showing a more comforting world or focusing on a character we would like to believe exists. We might fantasize about the life-style of a character like Magnum, wish for avengers like the A-Team, want to take a cruise on *The Love Boat*, and wish to believe in angels like Michael Landon.

3.   *Is the concept relatable?* Does the idea feature characters and circumstances we can accept as real? Except for news and documentaries, television does not deal with reality, but shows and characters must seem real to us. Most realistic primetime television programs are good examples of verisimilitude, the appearance of reality. Under these conditions, we can accept *M*A*S*H* as a realistic war drama-comedy, *All in the Family* as a realistic family comedy, *Hill Street Blues* as an inside look at a police precinct, *The Waltons* as an accurate depiction of life in the thirties, and *The Cosby Show* as a mirror of life in the eighties.

The Ability to Sustain the Concept over Many Episodes

One of the prime causes of failure in television series is the inability to sustain the premise over the three to five years necessary for financial success. Too often a network will commission a pilot that seems innovative only to discover later that it lacks the elements necessary to sustain it over time.

Network programmers frequently are attracted to a premise pilot— one that shows how the characters get together and sets the stage for the rest of the series. Unfortunately, it might be a poor indicator of what the series turns out to be. For example, some years ago ABC bought a half-hour comedy called *The Good Life*. The pilot was the story of a typical suburban couple struggling to earn enough money to pay the bills; they decide to throw in the towel and accept jobs as the chauffeur and maid for a wealthy millionaire. The couple moves to the estate, where they have their own cottage and can use the pool, tennis courts, and other facilities. As a wish fulfillment and highly relatable concept, it tested very well, and the network bought the series. But the concept of a middle-class couple disappeared after the pilot and the series quickly failed.

Having been burned by these experiences, network programmers want assurances that the expensive pilot they commission represents the series to come. NBC and ABC, which favor ninety-minute or longer pilot films, accept premise pilot ideas, as long as the entire pilot is not the premise. The rule of thumb is that the first half of the pilot can establish the premise, but the remainder of the film should represent a typical episode.

CBS, which prefers one-hour pilots, almost always rejects premise pilots. CBS executives insist that the pilot be written as if it were the eighth episode. If necessary, writers have been instructed to go back and construct the opening episode. NBC and ABC series almost always premiere with the pilot; CBS series frequently do not.

Internal Conflict Among Series Characters

An often overlooked but essential ingredient of both drama and comedy series is internal conflict. McCloud was unwanted on the New York police force and hated by his boss. Quincy was the bane of his superior's existence. Sergeant Bilko provided endless trouble for Colonel Nash. Archie and "Meathead" clashed on *All in the Family*, as did Hawkeye and Frank Burns on *M*A*S*H*.

Internal conflict fulfills important needs. Conflict is the simplest way of having characters express their feelings and attitudes. If all the continuing characters in a television series love each other, all they can do is smile and support one another. Not only can this be exceedingly saccharine, but it also is boring. It fails to provide dramatic conflict and to give viewers an insight into the lead characters.

Since conflict is the basis for all drama and comedy, the lack of any internal conflict means that some external conflict must be introduced in each episode. This means introducing an outside character whose problem is sufficiently exposed. One of the few successful ways of doing this is having the principal character(s) take on the guest star as a professional case. Clients come to a private detective, lawyer, or doctor to "spill their guts." Other familiar forms of exposition include the tape recording in *Mission: Impossible*, the phone call from Charlie in *Char-*

lie's Angels, and officials like Devon in *Knight Rider*, who brief their people (and the audience) on the case.

The strongest series concepts feature groups of people who ordinarily would not be friends or even associate with one another but who are trapped by circumstance. Such circumstances might be mandated (*M*A*S*H*, *Magnum, P.I.*), the result of filial relations (*All in the Family*, *The Cosby Show*, *Simon & Simon*), or work environments (*The Mary Tyler Moore Show*, *Moonlighting*). Regardless of the cause, these circumstances provide opportunities to explore each of the continuing characters and to provide sources of complementary stories featuring outsiders brought in for one episode. Typically, the producers and writers of a television series rotate through the cast; one week a *Miami Vice* story focuses on Crockett; the next week Tubbs is featured; occasionally there are episodes featuring Trudy or Switek and Zito. This is true for most successful series on network television.

SOURCES OF IDEAS

Where do ideas come from? The source of most television concepts usually is one of the following: current events, personal experiences of the creator, history, books and novels, feature films, or network-originated projects.

Current Events

The complex events that shape our lives often are the jumping-off point for new television series. Creators scan newspapers for ideas, especially human interest stories and profiles of individuals and businesses that are prominent in papers such as the *New York Times* and the *Wall Street Journal*. National and regional magazines also are rich sources of such material. Occasionally, even electronic "journals" ranging from *60 Minutes* to *P.M. America* and local versions of the same provide new ideas.

Personal Experiences of the Creator

Firsthand experience can be invaluable. Earl Hamner recreated his growing up in the thirties when he wrote *The Waltons*. He was the model for the lead character, John Boy. Producer Robert Cinader rode around with Los Angeles's then-experimental paramedic unit before creating *Emergency*.

In other instances, writers and producers have collaborated with an individual to use his or her life as the basis of a new series. Some years ago writer E. Jack Neuman used a real doctor as the model for Dr. Kildare, and a number of television police detectives have been based on real people.

History

Westerns, of course, have long used actual people and historical incidents as the bases for stories. Wyatt Earp, Bat Masterson, and Wild Bill Hickok come to mind. While period shows have been very successful in the miniseries format, they have had a mixed history of success as series. Nevertheless, history is a rich source of material and is seriously considered in the development process. The historical backdrop provides a unique visual experience for viewers and offers intriguing insights into life-styles and conflicts in different historical periods and political contexts.

Books and Novels

Series based on books and novels have become commonplace. Among the more successful have been *Peyton Place, Mickey Spillane,* and *Little House on the Prairie* (based on the works of Laura Engels Wilder). Less successful series ventures have included "Rich Man, Poor Man" (*Book II*), "Gibbsville," and *From Here to Eternity.*

While their value as literature may be questioned, comic books have formed a significant base for a number of successful television series. Everyone is familiar with *Superman, Batman,* and *The Incredible Hulk.* Of course, there have been a number of failures based on comic-book characters as well.

Feature Films

Network program executives are movie fanatics. They see most major (and not-so-major) films as soon as they are released. The networks have established office screenings of new films for their executives. Therefore, it is not surprising that movies are a common source of material for new television series.

Adapting a feature film to a television series has not always been successful, but that has not dampened the enthusiasm for this source. Successful ventures have included *M*A*S*H, How the West Was Won,* and *Eight Is Enough* (based on the book and movie *Yours, Mine and Ours*). The list of unsuccessful adaptations is long, ranging from *Planet of the Apes* to musicals such as *The King and I* and period dramas such as *From Here to Eternity*.

In many cases, movies have been the inspiration for a series of similar thematic intention. Thus, there were resemblances between *Star Wars* and *Gallactica*, *Raiders of the Lost Ark* and *Tales of the Gold Monkey*, *Animal House* and *Frat House*, and *Time Bandits* and *The Voyagers*, not to mention the many attempts to clone James Bond.

Network-Originated Projects

It has become a common practice for network executives, especially heads of programming, to conceive concepts, then turn them over to writers and producers for development. One of the more successful products of this collaboration has been *The A-Team*, created by Brandon Tartikoff, head of NBC entertainment, and developed by Stephen J. Cannell. Another successful action series, *Knight Rider*, was developed in this fashion. For every success, however, there have been disasters, such as *Supertrain* and *Manimal*.

DEVELOPING CONCEPTS

While most concepts for new series are pitched orally to network development executives, they usually are preceded by a written document. The benefit of putting a concept in writing is twofold. First, it provides an easy way to evaluate the elements of a concept and identify areas that need clarification or revision. Second, the written concept, when properly registered, provides legal copyright protection.

A fully developed concept for a television series contains three elements: a description of the arena or setting, character descriptions, and sample stories.

A Description of the Arena or Setting

The first section of a written concept should provide a description of the basic arena. Included in this description should be elements that illustrate unique and appealing aspects that make the concept desirable for a series.

Location often is the key element in a television series. Hawaii has

Figure 5–1. *Magnum, P.I.* is set in an exotic Hawaiian locale. Series star Tom Selleck is shown here with Ina Balin.

been found to be charming and desirable. San Francisco has been the setting of a number of successful shows. New York is interesting, New Orleans is colorful, and Miami is the new hot spot.

Other locales are less appealing. Chicago is attractive but difficult to film in the winter. Water (and underwater) shows are highly attractive but often too complex on a television budget and schedule. Rural locations can be spectacular, but because the networks are more interested in urban audiences, they are lukewarm toward small towns. British and European accents also have a bad track record with the networks.

Character Descriptions

Development executives have learned that the lead characters are the key element to any successful series. They separate a successful Hawaii-based show such as *Magnum, P.I.* from an unsuccessful venture such as 1984's *Hawaiian Heat*.

Concept submissions contain detailed descriptions of the leading characters, often including biographies that are rarely referred to in the pilot or subsequent series. Such detailed biographies, however, provide valuable insight.

Figure 5−2.   *Miami Vice* is set in a visually appealing southern Florida location. Actors Michael Talbot (left) and Edward James Olmos (right) are shown.

Casting often is discussed when preparing a concept. It is not unusual for a writer or producer to contact talent agents to determine whether a certain actor might be interested in the series. If the response is positive, the leading character might be molded after that actor to accommodate his or her interests.

In almost all situations, a prototype or model for the leading character is identified. These prototypes usually are well-established film stars or popular personalities who would never actually work in a series. Thus a leading character might be described as being "like Clint Eastwood," an "Eddie Murphy type," or a "new Goldie Hawn."

Sample Stories

The inevitable question raised by all concerned with developing a television series is how it will sustain through the years. What stories can be told the second year, the fifth year? The viability of a concept is measured by its ability to sustain over many episodes, without repetition. To demonstrate the many avenues a series might take, a number of story premises, no more than a paragraph each, usually are presented.

A concept almost always contains a brief description of the proposed premise story that begins the series. This story sets the characters in place and provides the jumping-off point for the series. In the concept stage, this story might be only a few pages in length. If the concept is accepted, it will be expanded, first to a detailed story outline and subsequently to a full-fledged pilot script.

TYPES OF PRESENTATIONS

The presentation of a concept begins with an oral pitch explaining the series idea. In most cases, the concept and character descriptions have been committed to writing, not only for copyright protection but also for evaluation purposes in the creative process. The written presentation usually is not shown to the network unless network executives have questions about the project or it is particularly complicated. In that case, the presentation is polished, printed, bound in an attractive folder with pictures or other visual material, and delivered to network programmers following the oral pitch.

Audiovisual aids occasionally are used in the pitch. When appropriate, maps, graphics, storyboards, pictures, and other materials are used. Sometimes these are left with network executives as a convenient and effective reminder of the project.

Videotape presentations also are gaining acceptance, especially if there is a need to simulate the look of the series. Although expensive, these video presentations usually are short—no more than ten minutes. In their most elaborate form, they might be animated storyboards, showing the main characters and types of adventures possible. More often these video presentations are compilations of stock footage, showing possible series locations. For a project based on World War II in the Pacific, Universal Studios prepared a videotape showing some of the footage available for the series.

One of the more elaborate video presentations helped sell _The Dukes of Hazzard_ television series. The creators of the project found an old B movie that had never played in large cities, recut the film, revoiced the characters, added a narrator, and presented a full prototype episode of the series. On the basis of that presentation, CBS bought the show.

Sometimes the visual aid is in the form of a live guest at the session. A clever developer who has enticed a well-known actor to become associated with the project can help sell the series by bringing the actor to the presentation session. While network executives have constant access to writers and producers, they rarely meet actors. Often they are as star-struck as members of the general public. Using a star to endorse a project can be a highly effective sales ploy.

Actors are not the only people brought to pitch meetings. One producer, Rick Rosner, sold *CHiPs* by bringing friends in uniform from the California Highway Patrol. Other experts, from psychics to karate experts and apes to robots, have been paraded through the offices of network executives. All this falls under the label of *showmanship*.

PITCHING A PRESENTATION

The procedure by which new ideas are presented to development executives varies little from network to network. If done properly, a new series can be presented and accepted within a half-hour's time.

The process begins with a phone call to schedule the pitch meeting. Since network development executives are busy, it might be a week or two before the meeting takes place. The phone call acts as a screening process for network executives. Individuals without representation often are rebuffed or referred to a subordinate. Networks are wary of discussing projects with people who are not properly represented, as the fear of lawsuits prevails.

Just before the meeting, all the participants assemble outside the office of the development vice president. The roster of individuals varies but usually includes the creator of the concept, the writer (if the creator is not a writer), and the creator's legal representation. If the creator works independently, his or her legal representative usually is an agent. If the individual has a contract with a studio or production organization, the representative is a studio development executive.

The network normally is represented by three people—the head of development, his or her assistant, and a junior member of the department who will record notes about the project.

The meeting always begins informally. The network executive usually tries to make the creative people feel at ease by initiating a short period of casual conversation. The development executive then brings the conversation around to the business at hand.

Usually the first person to speak is the agent or studio representative, who introduces the project in a general way and expresses confidence in the creative team and the concept, often indicating time periods on the network schedule where this show might be placed. Then the spotlight shifts to the creator, who proceeds with the verbal pitch. First, he or she describes the basic concept and presents arguments supporting the idea's merit. The creator explains how this project is different from present and past shows and describes how it allows for many different types of stories.

The creator then describes the principal characters in detail. Their biographies (which might never appear on screen) are revealed, along with their attitudes and quirks. Often a prototype actor will be mentioned. Only the primary characters are presented in detail; subsidiary ones might be referred to quickly or not at all. Often they are dismissed with a comment such as "and of course there are several other characters who will interact with the leads."

After presenting the basic idea and characters, the creator usually pauses for the network executives to respond. This response can take several forms.

1. The network executive in charge might express a lack of interest in the idea or inform the group that something similar already is in the works. If so, the meeting is over.
2. The network executive might ask questions. In this situation, the creator's response is critical. If a developer is asked to discuss some of the potential stories for the series, adequate preparation can spell the difference between acceptance and rejection.
3. The development executives thank the people for presenting the project. Sometimes a project is approved in the meeting, but usually the programmers end the meeting without giving a verdict.

Following this unwritten but established procedure, the development executives will mull over the proposal and meet to reach a consensus. One of them will then phone the project's representative (studio, production company, or agent) and inform him or her of the decision. This call usually occurs within seventy-two hours of the pitch session.

A number of key ingredients are necessary for a successful presentation. Among them are honest enthusiasm, abundance of detail, humor, conviction, and adaptability.

Honest Enthusiasm

It would seem superfluous to state that the presenter should be enthusiastic about the project. This is expected. It is crucial, however, that this enthusiasm be real and understated. Network executives are bombarded with sales pitches for "wonderful new series." If the presenter lapses into hyperbole, his or her credibility—and that of the project—will suffer. The key element is realistic enthusiasm.

Abundance of Detail

While some projects succeed because of slick salesmanship, the success record of such concepts is poor. A well-thought-out concept is rich in detail, covering most exigencies. Network programmers listen carefully for flaws in the concept to ascertain whether it has been carefully conceived.

Humor

What separates contemporary films and television shows from those of the past is humor. Examine the best of today's entertainment offerings, and you will discover a mixture of intense conflict and comedy. Consider Steven Spielberg's *E.T.* The film succeeds in putting the viewer through a roller coaster of emotions, from laughter to suspense to tears. The best television series do the same. Every contemporary concept, no matter how dramatic, should have humor. Levity in the presentation of any project is important as well. Network executives interpret the intensity and style of the pitch as a true indicator of the creator's stylistic intent.

Conviction

This should not to be confused with enthusiasm. The creator's determination to have this project accepted is vital to the presentation. People who are firm in their beliefs command respect. Conviction might not guarantee acceptance, but lack of conviction will encourage rejection.

Note that it is preferable for a creator to present only one idea per meeting. Since network meetings can be difficult to obtain and must be scheduled far in advance, there is the tendency to pitch several ideas per meeting. This presents some problems. The network might interpret the variety of ideas as a lack of conviction concerning one concept. It also puts executives in the uncomfortable position of choosing one idea over the others. Often they will respond by rejecting them all.

Adaptability

During the meeting, a network development executive often has suggestions about modifying the concept. Obviously, to reject such advice with comments such as "That's stupid" or "It won't work" is the quickest path to rejection. The least enthusiastic response should be "That's interesting. Let me think about it."

An open mind is crucial in such situations. It does not take much psychological training to understand that accepting an executive's modification gives that person a stake in the project and thereby increases its chances of acceptance. Moreover, development people often are concerned about the flexibility of creative people. Since television is a collaborative effort, it is easier to work with someone who is thoughtful and accepting of ideas than someone who takes any criticism as a personal assault.

6

From Concept to Pilot Production

As discussed in Chapter 5, deriving and presenting the concept is the first step in the progression from idea to series commitment. We have looked at the way ideas are formulated and how they can be turned into program presentations. In this chapter, we will look at the procedures that move ideas beyond the concept stage and into effective pilot stories and scripts. We also will look at the subsequent requirements for pilot production. Since ideas often are developed internally at studios and production companies, we will examine the strategies management uses to create successful concepts, stories, scripts, and pilots.

THE WRITTEN CONCEPT

As we have seen, a new series idea is designed to appeal to specific network interests, offering the potential of strong demographics, star power, and the ability to overwhelm the competition. For internal sales considerations, the network might be interested in seeing an extended series projection, which details future episodes and character descriptions. Most of the time, these projections are written by studio executives or production company executives. Once the network buys the series, those story projections usually are never referred to again.

When a show is purchased, a written concept is needed for internal network sales considerations. The written concept includes shorthand ideas about series longevity, lead character interest, and star appeal.

```
                           CONCEPT
                      MURDER, SHE WROTE




Angela Lansbury stars as celebrated mystery writer, Jessica

Fletcher, whose penchant for crime solving invariably

involves her in often-bizarre and always colorful escapades

Once a contented widow from a small town in Maine, Jessica

has found fame, as well as adventure, by turning her

avocational scribblings into a lucrative new career.  A star-

studded cast and an endless chain of nieces and nephews will

join her as she solves the most intriguing of crimes with

the most eccentric of methods.
```

Figure 6−1.   The written concept for *Murder, She Wrote.*

It also identifies the creative team responsible for overseeing development and production.

Figure 6—1, from the network presentation for *Murder, She Wrote*, gives you a sense of the brevity and style of a written concept. In this case, the star has been described, the intricacies of her character suggested, and the setting for the series laid out. In just one paragraph, the tone of the series is set, identifying Jessica Fletcher's penchant for solving bizarre crimes through eccentric methods. The presentation also includes a brief credit list for the key creative team: executive producers Richard Levinson and William Link (*Columbo*, "That Certain Summer," "The Execution of Private Slovik"), producer/writer Peter Fischer ("Once an Eagle," *The Eddie Capra Mysteries*), producer Robert O'Neill, and director Corey Allen ("Avalanche," *Simon & Simon, Whiz Kids*). Later in this chapter we will look at excerpts from the presentation script for this series.

Many times the concept sounds like a *TV Guide* marketing blurb, outlining the genre, series premise, and key characters. Many concepts are developed to meet specific network needs. NBC's Brandon Tartikoff sought a police show that would combine the excitement of high-action drama with the sound and pacing of MTV's rock video. In the hands of Universal Studios, writer Anthony Yerkovich, and producer Michael Mann, *Miami Vice* was born.

The sales presentation for *Miami Vice* (Figure 6—2) was written by Universal Studios executives, with the concept embedded in action, setting, and character interplay. In addition to the introductory concept, the presentation included a description of the lead characters, providing enough detail to relate the leads to the pilot story line. Once the series began production, the psychobiographies were all but forgotten (psychobiographies convey the background of characters in extensive detail).

Note how the *Miami Vice* concept plays up the elements cherished by the network: gritty police action, hot Florida setting, intense characters playing opposite each other ("theirs is an unholy and stormy alliance from day one"). The character descriptions also are integrated into the pilot story. To provide even more incentive for advertisers to believe in the series, the creative team was identified in separate pages: executive producer Michael Mann (*Police Story, Starsky and Hutch, Vegas*, "Jericho Mile") and executive producer/creator Anthony Yerkovich (*Hill Street Blues, Starksy and Hutch*). The team is strong, and their success in the genre has been proven.

Ironically, the show has moved in different directions than suggested in the pilot, including the addition of a new character—their steely-eyed lieutenant. The production stresses high visual values,

---

CONCEPT
MIAMI VICE

. . . An exciting new drama with the look of the 80.'s

. . . exploring the teeming world of vice amid the sunshine,

wealth, and waters of South Florida . . . narcotics, gun

running, smuggling, gambling, pornography . . . and the personal

lives of two cops who live on-the-edge and undercover . . .

CHARACTERS

SONNY CROCKETT

Ten years ago he was an All-American wide receiver for the

University of Florida "Fightin' Gators," He had a promising

gridiron career. But a knee injury sustained in an off-the-field

scrimmage with an agile majorette sidelined him from pro ball.

Though it may not be as glamorous as the NFL, Crockett has spent

the past 10 years as an undercover cop for the Miami Police

Department.

Crockett works out of a confiscated schooner at the Key Biscayne

Marina. He shares the yacht with his former football mascot -- an

---

Figure 6−2.   The concept and main character profiles for *Miami Vice.*

acid-freaked alligator named Elvis. With a $100,000 cigarette boat docked alongside and a Ferrari in the parking lot, Crockett seems like any other hard-partying ocean guide with a questionable means of support.

It's not a bad life if you don't mind scraping by on 4 hours sleep a night or living undercover for weeks at a time: dealer this month, outlaw biker the next, "If it's Tuesday I must be working drugs. . . ." And though he may appear unorthodox to the untrained eye, when it comes to being a cop he's strictly business.

Ricardo Tubbs

Drug dealers in Miami think he is a big-time Jamaican buyer with a thick patois and a taste for reggae. All Crockett knows is that he's partnered on this case with some hotshot vice cop named Rafael Tubbs on loan from the New York Police Department.

In truth, he is none of these things. He's a Bronx street cop who saw his older brother gunned down in an undercover drug deal that went sour. With forged police clearances, counterfeit money and "borrowed" IDs, Tubbs is in Miami to find and confront his

Figure 6-2. (continued).

brother's murderer, Colombian drug king Calderone.

Theirs is an unholy and stormy alliance from day one. Tubbs is New York, street wise, cosmopolitan and intense -- a sharp contrast to the laid back lifestyle of Crockett. Although new to the Miami drug scene, Tubbs survives with incredible bravado and coolness under fire. They are as different as North and South but share the same passion for justice.

And though he's not crazy about alligators named Elvis, motel living and Miami in general, he's got to stay. Like Tubbs says, after what he's pulled to get here, he couldn't get hired as a Bronx Meter Maid.

Figure 6-2. (*continued*).

Figure 6–3. Lighting is important to the production quality of *Miami Vice*. Here lights are checked for guest star composer Jan Hammer.

tones, pacing, and music, which is supposed to appeal to contemporary audiences.

PILOT STORY CONSTRUCTION

Once the concept has been developed, the basic arena for the series is set and the characters are refined to fit into the dramatic framework of the pilot story. In drama and comedy, the story outline itself is first presented orally, suggesting the major events and progression of the story and its climax.

How to prepare a premise story is a very real concern. Each network has a different philosophy concerning the best approach. CBS almost always insists on a pilot story that is a typical episode to convey how the series will play. NBC prefers premise stories that set the groundwork and introduce lead characters. ABC tends to mix it up, relying on both approaches. One-hour pilot stories can fall into either category, but a two-hour pilot is written exclusively as a premise story. It can then stand on its own as a television film, with its own *logline* for promotion. (A logline is a one-sentence description of the pilot.)

Before the project can move to the script stage, the story line must be approved by executives at the studio, For well-known writers, this approval might come without putting anything in written form. More often the story is expanded into a more detailed written form before it is approved.

The detailed story outline conveys the major dramatic action and conflicts for later embellishment. The broad elements of the story are told, with a clear beginning, middle, and end. The pilot story outline provides a clear picture of the story's unfolding premise, through character action, conflicts, and resolution of problems.

The story line sets the most effective plot structure for later development in the script. In the process of writing the story line, certain plot patterns become identifiable in the pilot show. One of these generally becomes dominant, while others serve as background or subplots in the script. It is interesting to see how some of these plot patterns relate to the thematic structure of a pilot story.

Some years ago, a critic named Georges Polti identified thirty-six dramatic plot situations that seemed to be at the heart of all dramatic stories. Later, Lewis Herman reduced the number of plot patterns to nine. Richard Blum discusses and analyzes these in *Television Writing: From Concept to Contract.** We have taken the liberty of embellishing, modifying, and merging some of these patterns, as well as adding some of our own to help identify certain generic stories.

These are some of the most utilized plot patterns in television: love and romance, fantasy, vengeance, jeopardy or survival, search or quest, group and family ties, return, and success and achievement. By no means is this list complete, but it does indicate the potential for dramatic conflicts faced by lead characters in a pilot story or script.

PLOT PATTERNS

Love and Romance

This kind of story deals primarily with romantic conflicts faced by lead characters and how they overcome those obstacles. Here is a traditional love pattern: Boy meets girl, loses her, must win her back. The story usually centers on a character's desire to maintain a loving relationship in the face of serious romantic problems. The story might draw on elements of the classic love triangle, in which an outsider enters into the

---

*Richard A. Blum, *Television Writing: From Concept to Contract* (Rev. ed., Boston: Butterworth Publishers, Focal Press, 1984), 79–80; Lewis Herman, *A Practical Manual of Screenplay Writing* (Cleveland: World Publishing, 1963).

romantic competition. Think of any primetime soap (such as *Dallas* or *Falcon Crest*), and you will notice that the love pattern helps sustain audience involvement with the lead characters.

Fantasy

In this pattern, characters confront their own weaknesses and are permitted to act out their fantasies on some level. In myriad variations of the Cinderella tale, lead characters become more complete as a result of their fantasy experience. Some of the more obvious shows in this genre are *Highway to Heaven*, *The Love Boat*, and *Fantasy Island*. These shows provide viewers with an outlet for their own fantasies.

Vengeance

Stories in the vengeance mode deal with lead characters who seek revenge for some wrongdoing. Characters in this type of story want to

Figure 6–4.   Some of the episodes in *The Equalizer* series are based on the vengeance pattern, with characters seeking help to overcome injustices. The series stars Edward Woodward.

solve mysterious crimes, get even for something, or simply right some earlier wrong. This type of story pattern is prominent in virtually every mystery, suspense, or action-adventure series, including shows such as *Murder, She Wrote, Miami Vice, Knight Rider, The Equalizer,* and *The A-Team.*

Jeopardy or Survival

The jeopardy pattern usually centers on a life-and-death situation, testing the survival instincts and prowess of the lead characters. In this story pattern, characters confront extremely difficult odds (such as an earthquake, avalanche, or hijacking). They use every mental and physical trick to overcome extraordinary obstacles. In some situations, those obstacles are compounded by a time bomb situation—that is, something must be done before time runs out and some disaster occurs. The classic series *Mission: Impossible* relied on this element, as does the contemporary show *MacGyver.*

Search or Quest

The search or quest pattern focuses on the notion of a person trying to find something of great importance. Sometimes the quest is external— searching for a missing witness, finding clues to a buried treasure, or looking for missing information. In that case, the search premise stands on its own as a story, but it also can be tied to larger story patterns such as vengeance or romance. On a more psychological plane, the search might encompass a character's drive to "find" himself or herself or to deal with a traumatic personal crisis. The external search provides a more action-packed framework, while the inner quest is more difficult to convey.

Group and Family Ties

This pattern involves a group of characters who normally would have nothing to do with each other but because of circumstances are tied together in the story. Primarily because of the locale, they are forced into interrelationships that become the focus of the story. These people might be in a hospital (*St. Elsewhere*), a police station (*Hill Street Blues*), a house (*The Golden Girls* or *The Cosby Show*), a bar (*Cheers*), a taxi dispatch center (*Taxi*), or an army camp (*M*A*S*H*). The basic story foundation is the same: A group of characters are bound together by their shared environment.

Return

Within one of the larger story patterns, a character might have to confront the sudden reappearance of someone or something from the past. This story element forces the character to readjust the comfortable status quo. For example, the lead character might be faced with the return of an ex-husband, high-school sweetheart, wandering father, missing child, long-lost lover, or long-forgotten criminal record. This pattern might serve as the basis of individual stories in the series, including the pilot, but generally it is not the overriding theme for a series concept.

Success and Achievement

Success is another story pattern that stands on its own but also fits comfortably into other patterns. In the success pattern, the lead character must achieve something at any cost. The goal might be self-serving (material, romantic, or vocational success) or altruistic. No matter what the goal, the character is nearly obsessed with the drive for success. He or she will stop at nothing to accomplish it.

A pilot story generally encompasses one or more of these story patterns to show how the characters will function in the script. The pilot script must show how the characters interract to accomplish their goals and must set them in the appropriate locale.

CHARACTERIZATION IN THE STORY AND SCRIPT

As we see in the *Miami Vice* proposal (Figure 6–2), lead characters are fleshed out initially to give a sense of the show's potential for ongoing conflicts. Character biographies serve as springboards for casting and story development. The more individualized the character, the more concrete the possibilities for casting and script development.

The pilot script, however, does not go into biographical detail about the character, except in the context of dramatic exposition. Instead, the script provides a simple physical sketch of characters (age, physical type) and conveys their personalities through actions, reactions, and dialogue. The script offers an opportunity for characters to interact uniquely on screen.

The development of unique characters is indispensable to a good story and script. If characters look and sound alike, the pilot will suffer. Even in the heat of romantic crises or a fast-paced car chase, characters must be consistent in what they do, say, and think.

One technique that helps identify realistic characterization is tied to the way actors interpret and analyze their roles. One of the more common approaches is grounded in variations of Stanislavski-based acting training. Stanislavski was the artistic director of the Moscow Art Theatre in Russia, and his techniques provided actors with tools for realistic character development. He brought those techniques to the United States in the early 20th century, and his impact on American stage and film has been legendary.*

Stanislavski's techniques, modified and criticized over the years, have played a prominent part in the way actors and directors approach a script. Writers, too, have learned the importance of testing the credibility of characters in their scripts. Using terminology from the Stanislavski-based schools (such as The Actors Studio), writers work toward more realistic and credible characters.** Some of the more important terms to consider are super objective, throughline of action, intentions, motivations, sense of urgency, state of being, and moment-to-moment realities.

Superobjective.   This is the main reason the character has been created. Each character, no matter how briefly he or she appears on the screen, has a major objective to accomplish. This differentiates each character from the next.

Throughline of Action.   This is a conceptual thread that shows how each character fits into his or her larger objective. Every time the character appears, an invisible thread connects him or her to past and future moments on the screen. This concept helps provide consistency throughout the script.

Intentions.   These are the behavioral actions of the characters in each scene. Intentions can change from scene to scene, and even within a scene if proper motivation is provided. Intentions usually are expressed as physical objectives—for instance, the character wants to steal a car, find a lover, or leave the room.

Motivations.   These are the inner drives that explain why a character must achieve a specific intention or goal. The psychological aspect provides a more well-rounded understanding of the character and has a unique impact on everything he or she does. A character does not have to

---

*For more on the Stanislavski system, see Richard A. Blum, *American Film Acting: The Stanislavski Heritage* (Ann Arbor, Michigan: UMI Research Press, 1984); Toby Cole, ed., *Acting: A Handbook of the Stanislavski Method* (New York: Crown, 1963); Christine Edwards, *The Stanislavski Heritage* (New York: NYU, 1965); Sonia Moore, *The Stanislavski System: The Professional Training of an Actor* (New York: Viking Press, 1960).

**For more on The Actors Studio, see David Garfield, *A Player's Place: The Story of the Actors Studio* (New York: Macmillan, 1980); Robert Hethmon, ed., *Strasberg at the Actors Studio* (New York: Viking Press, 1965); Robert Lewis, *Method or Madness* (New York: Samuel French, 1958).

undergo psychoanalysis, but it helps immeasurably for the writer to convey the wellspring of emotions and insecurities faced by each character.

Sense of Urgency.   A sense of urgency is tied into the character's intentions and motivations. It tells viewers how badly the character wants or needs to achieve some goal. The greater the sense of urgency, the greater the dramatic conflict. If a character desperately wants to achieve a goal and some obstacle is thrown in the way, the dramatic tension increases in direct proportion to that emotional intensity.

State of Being.   This ties the character into the physical and emotional framework of the scene. It encompasses the character's physical and inner states and provides viewers with a sense of consistency and credibility from scene to scene.

Moment-to-Moment Realities.   These are the character's reactions to everything he or she experiences in a scene. These realities take into account all the circumstances of the scene, including the impact of other characters, the physical environment, and the psychological realities of each moment.

The goal of any writer, producer, director, or actor is to create an appealing and enjoyable experience for viewers. Inherent in that goal is a respect for the importance of character development in the story, script, and production.

THE WRITTEN SCRIPT

Before the script is written, some writers develop a step outline, which clarifies the major action sequences for the show. The step outline details the visual and dramatic progression of the story, establishing appropriate plot points and character conflicts. Many other writers, however, feel that a detailed outline is restrictive, and they prefer to allow the story to play itself out in their minds. These writers usually are quite experienced and have a well-grounded understanding of teleplay dynamics.

In terms of structure, many shows begin with a short teaser designed to captivate viewers early. The script is then broken into several acts of approximately equal length, each ending at a point designed to hold viewer interest through the commercial break. A 30-minute script is broken into two acts; a 60-minute script has four acts; a 90-minute script has four to six acts; a 120-minute script has seven acts.

If the show is videotaped or shot like a situation comedy with multiple cameras, a different script format is sometimes used. The margins are much wider, and the dialogue and camera directions are double-spaced. The length of the script differs considerably from film. In film, each script page equates roughly to one minute of screen time. Thus, a 30-minute script is about 26 pages; a 60-minute show runs about 54 pages; a 120-minute script runs about 105 pages. In videotape, a 30-minute show is around 45 pages, with a teaser, two acts, and a closing tag. A 60-minute tape program can be 90 script pages or more. And a 120-minute script can require 180 pages or more.

Whether the pilot will be filmed or taped, the script must be well developed, introducing the characters at an early stage and maintaining viewer interest in the unfolding dramatic action or comedy events. The writer must handle problems of pacing, exposition, characterization, dialogue, and visualization with consummate skill. The pilot script conveys the atmosphere and locale of each scene and shows how characters act and react. The script is visually written to offer a concrete image of the locale, setting, and character action, as well as the general requirements for camera coverage.

Many first-draft film scripts are in a *master scene* form, which does not require the intricate technical information necessary in final shooting scripts. This form offers a vivid description of action within each scene but does not identify and number each camera shot. The master scene script conveys essential information concerning scene headings, scene descriptions, and character dialogue. Only a few technical terms appear. Among them are FADE IN, INT. OR EXT. LOCATION—DAY OR NIGHT, CUT TO, DISSOLVE TO, ANGLE ON, CLOSE-UP, BEAT, and FADE OUT.

FADE IN.   This is the first direction to be typed on all scripts. *FADE IN* means the upcoming picture gradually appears on the screen. The term is used at the beginning of scripts and at the start of each new act.

INT. OR EXT. LOCATION—DAY OR NIGHT.   The location heading specifies each new locale required for production. The set is identified as being interior or exterior, followed by a specific location and some indication of day or night lighting. These new scene headings help determine set design and location requirements, lighting requirements, and even rehearsal and shooting schedules for actors in the same scenes.

CUT TO.   This designates the end of one scene and the need to begin a new scene and location. It is a fast-paced scene transition.

DISSOLVE TO.   This also is used as a scene transition, but it is much slower paced than *CUT TO.* Technically, the dissolve is a superimposition of one scene on another, with the new scene gradually taking over viewer attention. The dissolve creates a mood or time transition effect.

ANGLE ON.   The angle usually is identified by a brief reference to the person or object focused on—such as *YOUNG WOMAN, CROCKETT AND RIVERA, LIMOUSINE.* It calls attention to specific people or perspectives. In some situations, the script simply calls for a *NEW ANGLE,* which suggests that another perspective is needed. The exact cinematic needs will be determined later by the director.

CLOSE-UP.   This is the full-frame coverage of a person's face or a specific object. Usually a *CLOSE-UP* of someone is accompanied by a description of that character's reaction to what he or she is experiencing.

BEAT.   This term is used to establish a moment's pause for the character to think or act in some way. It is the same as a Chekhovian dramatic pause—that is, a dramatic device for characters to take a moment or two before performing some action.

FADE OUT.   This is the converse of *FADE IN.* It is used to close out each act and to conclude the film. It usually is the last direction in the script.

Revising the Script

Every pilot script developed by a studio might undergo as many as three to five drafts before it is finally approved by studio heads for submission to the networks. The development executive reviews the project several times, offering extensive comments on each revision. In these script conferences, suggestions are made to strengthen dramatic focus, pacing, dialogue, characterization, and visual action. After production company executives are satisfied with the draft, they send it to the network as a first draft.

The network reviews the pilot script and decides that (1) the script is close to acceptance and can benefit from revisions or (2) the script is too far from acceptance levels, and the project is abandoned. If the project is worth pursuing, network and studio executives meet with the writer to go over suggested changes. These meetings can last up to two hours.

Once the second draft is approved by the studio heads, it is sent to the network for final evaluation. In essence, the network has two shots at the pilot script: first draft and second draft. It can approve or halt pilot development at either stage. Once the final draft is approved, preproduction begins.

#85928

THE MURDER OF SHERLOCK HOLMES

FADE IN

INT. AN OLD-FASHIONED GOTHIC LIVING ROOM - NIGHT

Moonlight streams in through a far window and we can hear
the sound of wind rustling in the streets. The window is
slightly ajar and swings back and forth causing an ominous
rattle. Suddenly we hear a sound -- a strangled cry -- and
then we begin to hear scratching -- as if someone is clawing
to escape. A beat, then a Young Woman appears at the head
of the staircase. She is dressed in a filmy negligee and
is carrying a candle. She listens attentively, almost
fearfully, knowing she has heard something but at the same
time, afraid to confront it.

                         YOUNG WOMAN
          Roger?
                    (beat)
          Roger, is that you?

Slowly she comes down the staircase. As she reaches the
bottom step, we again hear the rattle of the partially open
window swinging back and forth. The Young Woman's head
turns in that direction. She approaches the window, sets
the candle down. When she realizes the source of the noise,
she exhales a sigh of relief and latches the window securely.
But just as she does so, we again hear the muffled groan of
agony and the insistent sound of scratching. The Young
Woman's head whips around and she finds herself staring
at the door to the closet built beneath the staircase.

                         YOUNG WOMAN
          Roger?
                    (beat, intense)
          Roger, please. For God's sake -- if
          this is some kind of sick joke ---

The only response is another muffled groan of agony and we
can now barely make out the words -- "Help me -- please
help me." Slowly, terrified, the Young Woman approaches
the closet door. She hesitates with her hand on the knob,
then slowly and deliberately turns it. She slowly opens
the door and looks inside.

CLOSE - YOUNG WOMAN'S FACE

as she screams in terror.

Figure 6-5. Sample pilot script, for *Murder, She Wrote*.

#85928   2

HER POINT OF VIEW - CLOSE - A HOODED FIGURE

inside the closet, dressed in the garb of a Middle Ages
executioner. He holds an axe, raises it up over his head
and steps toward her menacingly.

NEW ANGLE

Screaming, the Young Woman turns and falls to her knees,
clutching at her chest, gasping for air. The hooded man
stands over her, axe held high, as she struggles for breath,
then collapse in a heap and lies very still. Hold for a
long beat, then we hear:

                          DIRECTOR'S VOICE
          And -- house lights!!!

At that moment, light suddenly floods the area. The
Executioner lowers the axe and whips off his mask as the
Young Woman rolls over and starts to get up.

ANOTHER ANGLE - FEATURING AUDITORIUM

We now realize that we have not been watching an actual
event but rather a stage play, specifically the final
moments of the first act of a play which the producers
believe is bound for Broadway but which is more likely
bound for blessed oblivion. The Director, an intense
little man in his twenties, bounds from his seat and
shouts at the actors.

                           DIRECTOR
          Too long! The first act is still too
          long! We've got to pep it up, people.
          All right, second act in ten minutes.
          Remember, we open tomorrow night. I
          don't intend to close the night after!

He moves to the back of the auditorium, suddenly spots
three women seated in the back row. He glowers as he
approaches them.

                           DIRECTOR
          Ladies, this is a <u>closed</u> rehearsal!
          No outsiders!

The lady nearest the aisle rises and smiles at him. Her
name is Jessica Fletcher, an attractive good-natured widow
in her middle years. Her friends are named Lois and Eleanor.

                           JESSICA
          Excuse me, Mr. Cellini, but you
          asked us to meet you here.

                            CONTINUED

Figure 6-5. (continued).

```
#85928                    3


CONTINUED
                          DIRECTOR
                Now why would I do a thing like
                that?  I don't even know you!

                          LOIS
                We're the refreshment committee ---

                          ELEANOR
                From the PTA.

                          DIRECTOR
                    (wearily)
                Oh, yes, yes, the cookie ladies.
                Please see me after the rehearsal.

                          LOIS
                Mr. Cellini, I just love the show --
                it's so -- mystifying.

                          ELEANOR
                It gave me goose bumps.

                          DIRECTOR
                    (beams)
                Ah, well, I'm so pleased.  You know,
                you ladies are a part of history --
                the first to see a brand new play
                brilliantly written by Sir Edmund
                Grover -- a true genius of the
                mystery genre.

                          JESSICA
                He certainly is.  And I'm sure no one
                in the audience will ever guess that
                the uncle is the killer.
                    (turns away)
                Well, come, girls, mustn't be in the
                way.

        They start to bustle off.


        DIRECTOR
                          DIRECTOR
                    (starting forward)
                Hey, wait a minute!


        NEW ANGLE - THE "LOBBY"

        which we will recognize as a corridor in the local high
        school.  In the b.g. we will see a large poster advertising
                                          CONTINUED
```

Figure 6-5. (continued).

#85928   4

CONTINUED

a "Pre-Broadway Premiere" of an "Exciting New Murder
Mystery!" entitled "SOMETHING TERRIBLE!" presented by the
Cabot Cove Players. The Director catches up with our
ladies as they start for the exit.

                    DIRECTOR
              (to Jessica)
         Hold it, lady! What ever made you
         think the uncle is the killer?

                    JESSICA
         Oh, he isn't? Well, then I was really
         fooled ---

                    DIRECTOR
         As a matter of fact, he _is_, Miss --
         uh -- uh ---

                    JESSICA
         Mrs. Fletcher. And this is
         Mrs. Hoey -- in charge of punch
         -- and Mrs. Thompson, brownies and
         macaroons.

                    DIRECTOR
         Charmed. Look, Mrs. Fletcher,
         somebody slipped you a copy of the
         script, right?

                    JESSICA
         Oh, _no_. But I _do_ love a good mystery
         -- and when the uncle showed up after
         the party with a different tie on, he
         must have changed it for a reason --
         and there was the phone call from the
         coroner -- he couldn't have known
         about that unless he'd overheard the
         doctor talking to the priest and of
         course, there was that whole business
         with the airline tickets -- But how
         silly, here I am explaining _your_ play
         to _you_. I'm so sorry. Come on,
         ladies. We'll watch the second act
         tomorrow with everyone else.

Jessica and the other two bustle off, leaving the Director
stunned and openmouthed. His disbelief slowly turns to
anger and he turns on his heel and strides back into the
auditorium, screaming!

                    DIRECTOR
         George!! Get me that idiot of a
         writer! I want to talk to him --
         now!!

                              DISSOLVE TO

Figure 6-5. (continued).

SAMPLE PILOT SCRIPTS

Let's look at the first few script pages from the presentation script for
Murder, She Wrote (Figure 6–5). The teleplay was written by Peter S.
Fischer, from a story by Richard Levinson and William Link, in association with Peter S. Fischer. Note how the scenes are visually described to
convey the essence of the place, the stylistic mood of the show, the
inherent atmosphere, and the pacing of the scenes. Characters are defined through their actions, reactions, and dialogue.

Even from these few pages, the script provides a fairly reliable sense
of the *Murder, She Wrote* series. At the beginning, the script provides a
brief teaser promising some suspense and introducing Jessica Fletcher's
character. In the next two pages, she is established as a crime-solving bon
vivant, having second-guessed the murderer in this "brand new" mystery play; needless to say, the stage director is beside himself. Only
after the visual teaser is established do we see Jessica sitting by her
own typewriter, busy at work on her ninth novel (the next pages of
script). The pilot shows how she becomes intricately involved in a
contemporary mystery and how she adroitly solves it.

Let's look at another example of the teleplay format. This time we
will look at the first few pages of the pilot for *Miami Vice* (Figure 6–6).
The script initially was called "Dade County Fast Lane" and was written
by Anthony Yerkovich. The pilot opens with Crockett undercover,
working in the gritty heat of Miami, enduring the hot rock music from a
break dancer nearby.

The entire script for the *Miami Vice* pilot is 85 pages. Even by
looking at a few pages, however, we perceive the mood. We are introduced to the ongoing visual and dramatic setting—hard, gritty characters in conflict; drugs, action, rock music, and the hot, muggy feeling of
southern Florida. In the script, the characters are integrally related
to the environment and to each other. The dialogue is harder than
what we read in *Murder, She Wrote*. In later episodes, dialogue is
clipped considerably to bolster the impact of visual sequences.

```
                        ACT ONE

FADE IN

EXT. GHETTO STREET CORNER - DAY - BREAK DANCER

Black, neoprene-spined, and all of sixteen.  Spinning, popping and
locking in the dog day triple-figure afternoon heat to the high-
decibeled shrieks of "Prince" on a monstrous ghetto blaster.  His
audience is comprised of a rather indiscriminate assortment of
neighborhood junkies and Robitussin freaks, and...

SONNY CROCKETT

A sandy-haired, blue-eyed male of wide-receiver dimensions,
disconsolately sucking a snow-cone at a nearby and unshaded hot
dog stand.  Dressed in jeans, t-shirt and well-worn Luccheses,
Crockett looks a cross between Lance Allworth in his prime and
an unemployed pot smuggler.  At the moment he is feeling every
moment of his thirty-four years as he squints up from his sports
section at the dancer's gyrations and...

                        CROCKETT
                    (winces)
              Five thousand street corners in greater
              Miami and Gumby here's gotta pick ours.

... to a good-natured Hawaiian-shirted Hispanic in his late
twenties by the name of...

RIVERA

Seated beside Crockett, glancing over towards the breaker with a
mouthful of rancid dog and...

                        RIVERA
                    (to Crockett)
              C'mon Sonny.  We're talking routine
              American street art.

                        CROCKETT
                    (back to sports page)
              Well at least he's not a mime.
                    (a thoughtful beat)
              I hate mimes.

                        RIVERA
                    (laughs)
              You're in a foul mood today.

Crockett responds with a loud and jaundiced blowing of his nose and..

                        CROCKETT
              I don't know why.  There's nothing I
              love more than hanging out in a two
              hundred degree heat wave with a
              terminal hangover and a flu bug,
                    (Cont)

                                             CONTINUED
```

Figure 6-6.   Sample pilot script, for *Miami Vice.*

2

CONTINUED

                         CROCKETT (cont)
                waiting on some third string brain-
                damaged coke runner.
                     (to dancer)
                Hey, shortstop, you wanna crank down
                the decibels a notch!?

Crockett winces in pain as the kid cranks up his blaster a good
10 percent. Rivera sympathetically hands him a tin of aspirin,
under...

                         RIVERA
                You sure he's going to show?

Crockett downs four aspirin with a mouthful of snow-cone sludge,
the cold sending his fillings up into his frontal lobe, then --

                         CROCKETT
                He better. I was up till 5 this
                morning trading shots of Cuervo Gold
                with the little bozo just to close
                the deal.

                         RIVERA
                     (a sympathetic nod)
                Be well worth it if he leads us to
                the Columbian.

Rivera breaks off at the sound of a car horn, whereupon both he
and Crockett turn to see --

CORKY FOWLER

A surfed-out blonde acid-casualty in his mid-twenties, Dade
County's answer to Jeff Spiccola, screeching up to the opposite
curb in a tasteless, shocking orange 450 SL convertible, under
which...

                         CROCKETT
                     (rising, to Rivera)
                Showtime.

Crockett and Rivera, carrying a briefcase, head across the sidewalk
for the 450, in the course of which...

CROCKETT

Passes a group of half-naked sunstroked neighborhood kids vainly
attempting to crank open a fire hydrant with an improvised lug
wrench. Crockett pauses to glance back at the ghetto-blasting
dancer in near b.g. then grabs the end of the wrench and...

                         CROCKETT
                     (to kids, mock recrimination)
                No respect for law and order.

                                        CONTINUED

Figure 6-6. (continued).

CONTINUED

3

-- with one deft wrench, cracks open the hydrant. A monumental geyser douses the junkies, break-dancer and delighted children alike, utterly short-circuiting the screaming ghetto-blaster as...

CROCKETT AND RIVERA

Jaywalk breezily across the street towards the 450, Rivera regarding his partner with ill-concealed amusement, under...

                    RIVERA
                 (sotto)
        So where'd I fly in from this time...?

-- as we --

                                        CUT TO:

INT. 450 SL - DAY - CORKY

Reacting to Crockett's intro of Rivera with...

                    CORKY
                 (blown away)
        Malibu!!!

-- as, radio blaring, he cranks a vicious left hand turn, traversing three lanes of traffic, and jams down A1A with Crockett and Rivera crammed uncomfortably into the passenger seat.

                    CORKY (cont)
                 (considering the implications,
                  to Rivera)
        Too much, Bobby! I mean, that's really
        far out, concept-wise.

                    CROCKETT
                 (bored, blows his nose)
        Don't strain yourself now, Fowler.

                    CORKY
                 (eyes brightening)
        No, think about it! Some underpaid
        beaner 20,000 feet up in the Andes picks
        two tons of coco leaves, hauls 'em by
        mule to a lab in Bogota out of which pops
        three keys of Peruvian marching powder
        that gets dieselled up to yours truly
        here in the sunshine state, who then
        turns it over, for an equitable profit,
        to your friend Bobby here, who wings
        it back to locust land!

                    RIVERA
                 (nodding, polite)
        Yeah. That's pretty far out all right.

                                     CONTINUED

Figure 6-6. (continued).

4

CONTINUED

                    CORKY
              (off their incomprehension)
     Don't you get it!?
              (beat)
     Malibu! Hollywood!! Couple g's of this
     stuff at least are bound to find their
     way to the silver screen up the hooter
     of one of those babes on Dynasty or
     Magnum or something, the reruns of
     which'll be seen five years from now on
     some battery-operated old tube by that
     same Peruvian beaner way down in the
     Andes!
              (suddenly screams)
     Man, I am freaking myself out!!

Crockett exchanges an utterly dazed look with Rivera as Corky settles
down with a quick one-and-one from a bullet-shaped vial, then cranks
a turn down a sidestreet.

                    CROCKETT
              (declining proffered coke)
     Where you going? My boat's at the
     Marina.

                    CORKY
     Not gonna need your boat, dude.
              (grins)
     Different stash. It's already in.

Crockett and Rivera exchange a surreptitious glance, pondering the
implications of this, then --

                    CROCKETT
              (turning down radio,
              nonchalant)
     You're still working for the Columbian
     though...?

Corky shakes his head with the self-satisfaction of the newly
incorporated, and grins...

                    CORKY
     O sole mio, Jimbo. Got a whole new
     supplier.
              (to Rivera, ala radio
              announcer)
     Now, factory wholesale! Direct to
     you the consumer.

                    CROCKETT
              (a beat)
     You sure that's smart?

                    CORKY
              (smiles)
     Free enterprise, dude. Basis of
     Western democracy.
                                        CONTINUED

Figure 6-6. (continued).

From Pilot Production to Series

7

Once a network approves a project for pilot, the process involves many more steps before the program ultimately becomes a member of that select group—primetime series. Each of those steps encompasses new problems and challenges faced by the producers and network.

PILOTS VERSUS PRESENTATIONS

There has been a long-standing debate about the necessity of pilot productions. Some argue that it is a waste of money and resources and that series decisions could be made at the script level. Alternatively, it is reasoned, the networks could simply order a number of episodes, put them on the air, and let viewer interest determine their worthiness.

Another alternative is the presentation film. Rather than expending the cost and effort of producing a full-fledged pilot, producers could make a short presentation of the series concept. This would include the stars and highlights from the show, much like a movie trailer previews a coming feature film.

The debate over the value of pilots stems from several considerations. First, the pilot is financially unrepresentative of the series. Due to the care and effort put into a pilot, its cost usually is two or three times the budget of a weekly episode. Moreover, the pilot might not offer a true representation of the series content. In a pilot, it is necessary to introduce all the main characters as well as tell a story. For that reason, most pilots are labeled premise pilots. The pilot for *Trapper John, M.D.* had him joining the hospital staff. In *Miami Vice* Crockett met Tubbs for the first time. These pilots must introduce the series characters to one another and establish their relationship and the physical location for the series.

Sometimes, however, the premise is more interesting than the series that ensues. One of the most bizzare premise pilots occurred a number of years ago with a quickly forgotten series called *Sarge*. In the pilot, George Kennedy stars as a policeman whose wife is killed by a trap set for him. He is so distraught by the event that he quits the force and becomes a Catholic priest. But when clues show up pointing to his wife's murderer, he becomes a quasi-cop who finds and arrests the killer. It made an absorbing and emotionally arresting pilot film, which was bought as a series. The series, however, turned out to be the adventures of a priest who acted like a cop. While it told a number of interesting stories and was intelligently produced, the series quickly sank because of its unbelievable and unwieldy premise.

While the criticism of pilots has some validity, most network programmers believe that those weaknesses are outweighed by other considerations. With respect to the idea of presentation films, they argue that attractive presentations only demonstrate the ability of the creative people involved to produce a good trailer, not a series. Presentations are like advertisements. They sell the good points but cover up the flaws. Some producers are experts at producing flashy, humorous, and exciting twenty-minute presentations. They are considerably less adept, however, at overseeing full series productions. From time to time, series have been bought from presentations, often with less than successful results.

Putting Together a Pilot

Because pilots are extravagantly produced, they show the actors and characters in their best light and demonstrate the kind of stories that could be told in the course of a series. Since most series television succeeds or fails on the basis of its characters, the delineation of characters in the pilot is crucial to the programmer's selection process.

Production of a pilot is much like building a prototype of a new aircraft or testing the design of a new car. It is the opportunity to make mistakes and correct them. Pilot production entails the cooperative effort of a group of people who have never worked together, from the producers to the stars, film, crew, and postproduction editors. Like the tryout of a Broadway show, it is a tumultuous crucible where some people work wonderfully and others must be replaced; where ideas that looked good on paper become disastrous on film; where beauties become beasts and ugly ducklings become swans. Production turns an elusive idea into a concrete form, often with results that surprise the producers as well as the casual observer.

No producer ever sets out to make a bad television show. It does happen, but not because of lack of effort or dedication. The pilot process is a period of testing, luck, and, most importantly, learning. After a pilot has been produced, the creative team has gained vital knowledge about how to produce the series and make it even stronger.

Why Some Pilots Fail as Series

If the pilot process is so valuable, why do so many series fail? A number of factors come into play, from creative changes in the series to inopportune scheduling by the network. The lessons learned from pilot production can be lost in making the series. Sometimes the person responsible for the pilot does not produce the series. In every case where the key creative individuals responsible for the pilot are unavailable for the series, the probability for series success is much lower.

Another problem is network requests for content changes. Frequently, the network buys the pilot but then asks for changes in the series approach. If there is a radical change between pilot and series, many of the lessons learned during production of the pilot are no longer valid.

Most program development executives agree that the best running length for a dramatic pilot is ninety minutes. This allows adequate time to initiate the premise for the series, introduce the main characters, and tell a compelling story. Unfortunately, networks find that scheduling a ninety-minute pilot is cumbersome, usually requiring them to preempt an entire evening's schedule to broadcast two pilots back-to-back.

As a result, most pilots are either one or two hours long. Two-hour pilots often seem stretched. It is difficult to find a story big enough to occupy the time yet small enough to inaugurate the characters. One-hour pilots are exercises in condensation. It is difficult to introduce the premise and characters and tell a significant story in the forty-six-minute running time of a primetime hour.

Studios and producers usually prefer a longer pilot if given the choice because it allows them to make a more significant film with good production values. Due to efficiencies of production, the cost of a two-hour film is only one-third more than the cost of a one-hour pilot. Further, the success ratio of two-hour pilots is substantially higher than that of one-hour pilots. The longer forms are advertised as major television events and thus are given special promotional consideration. Two-hour pilots often are shown in network movie time periods, where they are promoted as premiere films and are treated almost like full-length feature presentations.

NETWORK APPROVAL RIGHTS: THE BATTLE OVER CREATIVE CONTROL

The networks have demanded and received certain approval rights, ostensibly to protect their investment. They have obtained exclusive rights to the property and pay for most if not all the cost of production. As a result, they want to oversee the full spectrum of creative activity. This demand for control has evolved into an ongoing battle between the network and creative community. Negotiations usually lead to a cumbersome compromise. Too often, the unhappy result is an uninspired pilot that never becomes a series.

Some projects are never produced because of conflicts over the right of approval. Imagine the frustration of a writer, having gone through the process of pitching an idea, getting it approved, writing a script in its many drafts, and having the final version approved to pilot—only to have the network disagree on the star's acceptability. The writer/producer knows the project intimately but is unable to settle on a star who meets his or her creative instincts and the network's desire for an acceptable name.

The network's approval rights fall into four categories:

1. The lead actors
2. The director
3. Final acceptance of script revisions
4. Compliance with the broadcast standards department

The Lead Actors

Since it is well known that the success of series television is heavily dependent on the leading characters, it is not surprising that the networks are very concerned with the actors who are selected. While there is always a desire for widely known personalities, it is understood that series television often makes its own stars. No poorly conceived or executed series has ever survived simply because it starred some famous person. Indeed, the reverse often is true.

If there is an advantage in having a known performer, it is in comedy, where the concept of the show often is considerably less important than the personality of the lead character. Having a major performer such as Bill Cosby can be a big asset in determining the success or failure of a series.

In drama, however, this is rarely the case. Most successful dramatic series have starred unknown actors who became famous because of their role in a successful show. Indeed, many of them experienced failure in earlier television attempts. Tom Selleck appeared in several unsold pilots and a few short-lived series before becoming the lead in *Magnum, P.I.* Don Johnson was labeled a has-been because of repeated failures in several short-lived series prior to his becoming Crockett in *Miami Vice.*

Given the importance of leading actors, it is reasonable to ask why casting deliberations occur so late in the development process. First, during the formative process of creating a concept and writing a pilot script, prototype actors for the lead roles often are discussed. Usually these are "wish" actors—that is, stars whom the network and creators would love to hire but who are unavailable or uninterested in working for series television.

Why Some Actors Avoid Series

It is understandable that major motion picture actors will not work in television series. They command immense salaries and do not want to put up with television's faster pace, longer hours, and often more difficult schedule.

What is surprising is the number of actors, barely recognizable by the general public, who refuse to work in series television. There is a class system in Hollywood, with motion pictures at the top, followed by miniseries and television films. At the bottom of the hierarchy is series television. Many actors feel that they can earn a sufficient living by working bit parts in motion pictures and taking roles in television movies and miniseries rather than working in a television series.

One major drawback to accepting a regular role in a television series is the long commitment it requires. Contracts usually are written for five to seven years, even though few series last that long. The seven-year contract ensures that the original cast will remain intact if a show is successful. The contracts do not prevent actors from working in motion pictures or miniseries. Since most series begin production in July and do not finish the season until March, however, there are only a few months when actors are free from the heavy grind of ten-to twelve-hour days during the production season. Like anyone else in that situation, many actors prefer to use part of that time for a vacation.

The Casting Process

The process of selecting actors for continuing roles begins after network acceptance of the pilot script and the assignment of a casting director to the project. The casting director might be an in-house person at a major studio or a free-lance director. After lengthy discussions with the producer and a brainstorming session with the network casting department, the casting director compiles a list of prospective candidates. He or she then contacts these actors' agents, and the interested actors are invited to meet with the producer and director. Meanwhile, the casting director continues to search for other candidates.

Casting sessions can be time-consuming and tedious for all parties. Actors are given a few pages from the pilot script and are asked to read for the producers. An actor coming into a casting session typically will find the following situation.

The waiting room is already filled with actors trying out for the same role and other roles in the pilot. After a wait of indeterminate length, the casting director ushers the actor into a room filled with people, including the producer, the director, and others on the production staff. The actor is introduced, and a short discussion follows, usually focusing on the actor's most recent work. Often the actor will pass out an eight-by-ten glossy picture of himself or herself with credits on the back. The producer then asks the actor to read.

The actor is placed in a position visible to the production jury, and the casting director reads the other characters' lines. The scene usually lasts less than five minutes. When it is done, the producer thanks the actor, who is quickly replaced by the next person in line. Subsequently, the casting director tells the actor whether he or she is still in the running or whether it is time to look for other work.

Casting is a simple winnowing process. Those performers who pass the initial test are earmarked as finalists. The finalists have to pass a second test—reading for the studio or production company. The four or five actors accepted by the producer are asked to repeat their readings for the studio executives in charge of development. At this point, the studio executives might feel that none of the performers is acceptable and send the producer and casting director back to find new prospects. Or they might feel that all the candidates are good. More likely, they will narrow the choices down to two or three people.

Having survived this round, the finalists are taken to the network, where they perform their readings for the network casting department and the heads of programming. This can be a large, intimidating group consisting of the head of programming for the network, his or her assistants, the heads of development, the studio chiefs, the casting personnel of the network and studio, and finally the writer, director, and producer of the project.

One by one, the finalists are paraded into the room and again read their part (the casting director plays the other roles). Once the actors leave, the group attempts to reach some consensus. Among the possibilities are the following:

1. An actor is selected for each of the major roles in the pilot. The project is approved to film.

2. There is some doubt that the proffered actors for one or more of the roles are suitable. This is resolved by arranging for film or videotape tests of the actors and looking at their work at a later time.

3. The network rejects all the prospects for one or more of the roles. This generates discussion about other candidates and sends the casting director and network casting department scurrying to find new prospects for the role(s).

Sometimes an actor who has been rejected at an earlier stage of the selection process is rejuvenated, but this is not a frequent occurrence. More often the casting process starts over with a redefinition of the qualities desired for the role.

There are times when the inability to find the right actors postpones a project for six months to a year. On occasion, the inability to agree on casting delays a project so long that it is ultimately abandoned.

The Director

It is generally recognized that television is a producer's medium, while motion pictures are a director's medium. In motion pictures, the director almost always sets the pace, has control over the script, chooses the production team, and supervises the postproduction process, even to the point of choosing advertising campaigns for the film and checking the sound systems of important theaters, as do George Lucas and Steven Spielberg.

In television, the producer is clearly in charge. The director is relegated to the position of a high-priced traffic cop. His or her main responsibilities are providing sufficient angles and close-ups to allow the producer to cut and postproduce the film, maintaining the production schedule, and replicating the shooting script. The director's participation in revising the script or changing scenes is limited.

Nevertheless, the director is vital and can spell the difference between a brilliant production and a weak one. The quandary faced in television production is that although the director is not a key member of the group spearheading the project, directing can be the difference between success and failure.

Consequently, the selection of the right director is crucial. A director must have an affinity for the project without wanting to change it markedly, must be able to achieve a unique look under the constraints of television scheduling and budgets, and must be supportive and subservient to the producer and writer.

Normally, a director is chosen shortly after the project is given the green light to proceed to production. This enables the director to have input during the casting process, as well as in choosing locations, crew members, and art directors. Like the selection of the cast, the choice of director can be a tedious process of compromise.

The best television directors have their choice of projects. They are sent many pilot scripts and can choose the ones that interest them. The producer and writer also can have an effect on a director's decision. Since television is such a collaborative medium, a good working relationship with the producer and writer are important.

The producer normally compiles a list of directors he or she would like and submits this to the studio or production organization. Thus begins the process by which a director must run the gauntlet. If the director is known to be difficult, or more importantly to have flagrant disregard for financial and time constraints, the producer will have a hard time convincing the studio to approve the individual.

Figure 7–1.   The director has input into casting and choosing location, crew, and art director.

The directors deemed acceptable are sent to the network programming executives for their approval. As with casting, the network might approve one or more of the people suggested, might offer additional suggestions of its own, or might reject all the prospects. If the latter is the case, then the producer must suggest other candidates. It is not uncommon to have projects delayed for weeks, even months, because the only directors acceptable to both the producer and the network are either not interested or not available. As yet, however, no pilot project has been abandoned because of the inability to agree on a director. Sometimes, however, the compromise choice acceptable to both parties is a poor one, leading to the ultimate failure of the pilot.

Final Acceptance of Script Revisions

Networks also insist on final acceptance of script revisions. It might seem that once a script has been selected for pilot, revisions become a secondary consideration. This is rarely the case, as a number of factors intervene. Among the most significant are economic considerations, locations, network concerns, and lead actor(s).

Economic Considerations

The writer of a pilot script is aware that he or she must remain within a rather limited budget. Little attention is given to the actual cost of producing the pilot, however, until it is approved to film. Since the creative people recognize that this pilot is going to determine the success or failure of the project, they tend to want to make it as flashy as possible. Distant locations, special effects, and spectacular stunts are almost de rigueur.

The free form of writing the pilot script soon clashes with the cold reality of television budgets. The economics of television demand that the production company or studio bear some of the cost—and thereby some of the risk—of making the pilot. In the case of a two-hour film, this can amount to a million dollars or more. If the network does not buy the project, which is usually the case, the producer has little opportunity to recover much of this money. The network, however, can always play the pilot as a television movie and recoup a substantial portion of its investment.

This very real issue of cost, and the size of the deficit the production company can absorb, has scuttled more than one project. It is not unusual for a network programming department to approve a pilot, only to find out later that the cost is too high. In such cases, it is easy to empathize with the creator and writer, who have gone through the entire development process, only to have the project abandoned as an economic albatross.

Locations

Often tied to economic concerns, but frequently a separate issue, is the matter of where to shoot the pilot film. The outline of the script might have placed the action in some exotic locale such as Hawaii or in some exciting city such as Chicago or San Francisco. When the real world of bad weather, high costs, permits, and availability of accommodations enters the picture, these locations frequently are abandoned, replaced with a similar substitute, or faked through the judicious use of stock footage combined with local sites. Many a film placed in Hawaii got no closer to the islands than Santa Barbara and a film vault. Similarly, the San Pedro district of Los Angeles, combined with the right stock footage, has substituted for San Francisco in many television films.

Network Concerns

Since the pilot script has already surmounted the hurdles of story and first-draft approval, network demands for rewrites are minor at this stage of production. Usually network discussions focus on changing the attributes of a particular character or clarifying the story's logic.

Figure 7–2. Shooting on location adds a sense of realism but also increases the cost of a television show. This is a scene from *Knight Rider*.

Lead Actor(s)

It is natural that once a star performer has been selected and accepted for the lead role, the script should be modified to suit that individual. The actors themselves often are brought into these discussions so that they feel more comfortable with the role and enthusiastic about the portrayal. For example, the Jessica Fletcher role in *Murder, She Wrote* originally was conceived for Jean Stapleton. When Stapleton decided that she did not want to work in another series, the producer, Peter Fischer, and Universal Studios were fortunate to get Angela Lansbury. The pilot script was then revised to reflect Lansbury's personality.

Compliance with the Broadcast Standards Department

The broadcast standards recommendations made during script development might not be given full consideration during the early drafts. They must be addressed, however, and any problems must be resolved before the project is approved for production. Sometimes this leads to bitter arguments among the writer, producer, and broadcast standards executives, with a fervent appeal to development executives to intervene. Because the broadcast standards department is a separate entity within the network, this can be a sticky situation.

Broadcast standards problems are almost always resolved in one of the following ways:

1. Some compromise action or dialogue is agreed on.
2. The questionable material will be filmed or taped in two versions—one to satisfy the producers, the other to satisfy the censors. The decision as to what is allowable and what must be cut is then deferred until the film is completed.
3. The producers give lip service to the broadcast standards executives and then proceed to shoot the film the way they want. This almost always generates a crisis during postproduction, when the broadcast standards executives must approve the film before the network will accept or pay for it. The producer then faces reshooting, reediting, or letting the standards executive in charge physically cut the offending scene out of the picture, whether it affects continuity or not.

A particularly harsh example of a broadcast standards memo was sent to Chris Crowe, producer of a television movie entitled "Streets of Justice." The memo is reproduced in Figure 7-3. When such concerns are finally resolved, the project proceeds to actual production.

NBC National Broadcasting Company, Inc.   3000 West Alameda Avenue
                                                 Burbank CA 91523 818-84... 3...

Warren J. Ashley
Broadcast Standards
Program Policy Manager

April 19, 1985

Chris Crowe
UNIVERSAL CITY STUDIOS, INC.
Tower - 12th Floor   VIA MESSENGER
100 Universal City Plaza
Universal City, CA 91608

RE: STREETS OF MALICE
     aka DEADLY FORCE
     aka POINT BLANK

Dear Chris:

Please be aware that the following language screened in the
dailies for the project noted above is not acceptable and
should not be included in the program when it is delivered to
NBC: "Fuck it," "Goddamn," "Goddammit," "Jesus," "Waste the
muther," "scumbag," and "ass hole."

Also, the shot of Zero unbuckling his chaps prior to entering
the car is unacceptable and should not be included in the
program.

Sincerely,

Warren Ashley

WA:rap
3009C

cc: A. Beaton, C. Balian, R. Lindheim, A. Shayne,
     S. Whittaker

     M. Brustin, J. Bures, R. Daniels, R. Dewey,
     R. Gitter, M. Goodman, W. Littlefield, M. Marshall,
     K. Wendle

Figure 7-3. Sample memo from broadcast standards department to
the producer of a television movie titled "Streets of Justice."

THE ACTUAL PRODUCTION PROCESS

The Production Budget

While final creative elements of the pilot are being handled, the business affairs departments of the network and production company are haggling over the considerable cost of the pilot. In 1986 the budget of a one-hour film pilot hovered around the two-million-dollar mark, and the expense of a two-hour film almost always exceeded three million dollars.

In one sense the battle between the network and producing entity over the cost of the pilot can be likened to the discussion between a car salesman and a prospective buyer. The buyer (network) wants the film for as little as possible; the salesman (studio) would like to make a profit. But the similarity ends there because of two other major factors.

First, there are three networks and therefore only three buyers. Second, the networks realize they are buying the show for two runs, after which all rights revert back to the producing entity. For that reason, the network never pays for the full cost of the pilot. The bartering revolves around how much loss or deficit the producing company can and will absorb in the project. It is not uncommon for the studio to spend a million dollars more than the network pays for a two-hour project. At times the cost has run as high as several million dollars because of bad luck or bad planning.

Obviously, a production schedule is made and a proposed budget calculated before the bartering process between network and supplier begins. The outcome of these negotiations determines the actual budget and shooting schedule of the pilot and almost always entails further revision of the script.*

For a major studio like Paramount or Universal, the cost of a typical day of production in 1985 amounted to approximately thirty thousand dollars. Therefore, compressing the shooting schedule can have an enormous effect on the total cost of the project. Some of the ways this is done follow:

1. Reducing the number of locations so that a number of scenes can be shot in one place without taking the time to move to another location.
2. Changing night scenes to day scenes, which usually are cheaper to shoot. If night scenes are required, they might shoot "day for night,"

---

*For a sample production budget, see Chapter 12.

meaning that night scenes are shot during the day, with special attention to lighting requirements.

3. Eliminating locations.
4. Using second-unit crews for chase or action sequences, with photo doubles for the actors. Second units can shoot additional scenes on location while the main scenes are shot elsewhere.
5. Eliminating scenes with large crowds of extras that consume time and money.
6. Consolidating and eliminating peripheral characters.
7. Eliminating, contracting, or simplifying sequences requiring action or special effects.

The Production Schedule

The delivery date demanded by the network also dictates schedule considerations. In the past five years or so, the networks have ordered their pilots in January, requesting that they be delivered in final form by the middle of April. For two-hour pilots, particularly those that require special effects, exotic locations, or considerable action, this is precious little time for finalizing projects that have taken six months or more to create and write.

Actual production on a long-form pilot might not begin until March. On many occasions, filming is finished only a week or two before the required delivery date. This jeopardizes the finished product considerably, as the postproduction process is abbreviated.

Some pilots are not completed before the network scheduling deadline. In these instances, the producers cut together a presentation of highlight scenes from the pilot. Various techniques are used to bridge the missing sequences; sometimes narration is employed, while in other instances small segments are shot exclusively for continuity. The finished product often looks so good that test audiences are unaware that they are viewing a condensed version of the pilot.

In some cases, the condensations are too good. Networks have become wary of ordering series from presentations. On occasion they have found that the full pilot is not nearly as well paced and interesting as the presentation. Nevertheless, a number of highly successful series have been bought on the basis of an incomplete pilot, including *Murder, She Wrote* and *Knight Rider*.

The Shooting Schedule

No matter the length, every program must have a shooting schedule. The shooting schedule breaks down the script into the production requirements for each day. Among the categories are sets, cast needs (stars and atmospheres or extras), page counts (lengths of scenes), vehicles or props required, and day or night lighting requirements.

A sample shooting schedule from an episode of *Simon & Simon*, a one-hour action series, is shown in Figure 7−4. The full schedule is ten pages long, encompassing seven days of shooting. The figure shows the first two days of shooting requirements.

All actors and crew members are notified in advance of daily scheduling requirements. A *shooting call* summarizes each day's requirements. A sample shooting call from another episode of *Simon & Simon* is shown in Figure 7−5. The crew was to report to the location at 7 A.M. The page count (number of pages to be shot) is listed, the set is described (exterior high school, exterior high school lawn, interior high school utility room). The scene numbers are listed, as are the day and night lighting requirements. Note that the cast (lead actors and bit players) are told where and when to report for pickup or shooting. The atmospheres and stand-ins are told where to report in a separate list. *Atmospheres* are extras (students, chefs, waiters). *Stand-ins* are actors hired to double for the lead actors. The advance information in the call refers to the following day's needs. In Figure 7−5, every technical requirement is listed for that day's shoot, from camera and sound to food services and transportation. Figure 7−6 shows *Simon & Simon* costars Jameson Parker and Gerald McRaney.

The Importance of Dailies

After the months of planning prior to filming, you might think that last-minute revisions and changes would be rare. Unfortunately, that is not the case. As the vision of the script is translated into the concrete form of videotape or film, glaring errors often become apparent. Usually they are spotted during the viewing of the dailies—the film shot the previous day. Dailies are scheduled principally for the producer and the editors so they can monitor the progress of the shooting and begin making editorial choices for the finished product.

Dailies also offer a preview of the finished film and therefore are given careful consideration by the studio and the network program executives. Evaluating dailies is a difficult task, and most people who try to ascertain how the finished production will look on the basis of dailies are deceived. It is easy enough to judge whether the camera is placed properly, whether the actors are delivering their lines well, whether there is sufficient coverage (different views of the same scene), and whether the film is in focus. It is far more difficult to judge the emotional viability of the scene and ascertain a sense of pace.

SHOOTING SCHEDULE

SIMON & SIMON

Prod. No. 62204   Director: GERALD McRANEY
Title: "The Cop Who Came to Dinner"   Ass't. Director: PAUL CAJERO
Start: 7/14/86   Unit Manager: JIM GARDNER
Finish: 7/22/86 (Camera Days - 7)

DAY/DATE	DESCRIPTION OF SET	CAST & ATMOS	PAGES	VEHICLES LIVESTOCK PROPS	DAY or NITE
1ST DAY MONDAY 7/14/86 STAGE 18	INT. A.J.'S HOME Scs. 34,35 Brown finicky over accommodations.	A.J. RICK BROWN ATMOS 3-standins	2-4/8	Imported ham Brown's cast Crutches Rollaway bed N.D. refrigerator supplies Blankets Linen Frozen chimichongas Provolone cheese Jarlsberg cheese Gouda cheese Fontina cheese Gorgonzola cheese	D-2
	INT. A.J.'S HOME Sc. 45 Rick yanks Brown inside from patio.	RICK BROWN ATMOS 2-standins	3/8	PROPS: Crutches	D-2
	INT. A.J.'S HOME Sc. 48 A.J. returns with food. Brown disconsolate over Temple.	A.J. RICK BROWN ATMOS 3-standins	1-1/8	Grocery bag Danish ham Muenster cheese German beer Kosher rye bread	D-2
	INT. A.J.'S HOME Sc. 56 Brown insists that both Simons go on stakeout.	A.J. RICK BROWN ATMOS 3-standins	1-4/8	2-bottles beer Bills Crutches	D-2

(1ST DAY CONTINUED)

Figure 7-4.   Shooting schedule for *Simon & Simon*.

-2-

DAY/DATE	DESCRIPTION OF SET	CAST & ATMOS	PAGES	VEHICLES LIVESTOCK PROPS	DAY or NITE
1ST DAY MONDAY 7/14/86 (CONT'D) STAGE 18	INT. A.J.'S HOME Scs. 85,86 pt,87 Cecilia lays "Temple" guilt trip on Brown.	A.J. CECILIA BROWN 3-standins	2-6/8	Porch chair Stain & brush Canvas drop-cloth Cake pans Sauce pan "Okra" dinner Crutches SPEC. EFX: Practical stove	D-3
	EXT. ST./INT. POLICE STATION Stills of younger Jenkins and wife.	JENKINS ATMOS 25-year-old wife 1-standin	-	MAKE-UP/HAIR Build up nose Beard & moustache as discussed VEHICLES: Red Porsche NOTE: Stillman	D
END OF 1ST DAY			TOTAL PAGES: 8-2/8		
2ND DAY TUESDAY 7/15/86 INTERNATIONAL AUTOMOTIVE, 10637 MAGNOLIA, NORTH HOLLYWOOD NOTE: 2-CAMERAS	EXT. GARAGE Scs. 1,2,3,4,9,10,11,12 Brown tries to shoo away Simons as informant pulls up.	A.J. RICK BROWN NIXON NIGHT CRAWLER 4-standins	2-7/8	PROPS: Acetylene torch Welding masks 2-baseball tickets VEHICLES: Dismantled pickup Power wagon Crawler sedan SPEC. EFX: Bumper rigged GRIPS: 1-add'l grip WARDROBE: Steel tip shoes CAMERA: 2-camera crews	D-1
(2ND DAY CONTINUED)					

Figure 7-4. (continued).

-3-

DAY/DATE	DESCRIPTION OF SET	CAST & ATMOS	PAGES	VEHICLES LIVESTOCK PROPS	DAY or NITE
2ND DAY TUESDAY 7/15/86 (CONT'D) INTERNATIONAL AUTOMOTIVE, 10637 MAGNOLIA, NORTH HOLLYWOOD	EXT. GARAGE Scs. 14,15,16,20A,20B,20C,20D, 20E,20F,20G Brown shot at and run over.	A.J. RICK BROWN NIXON NIGHT CRAWLER JENKINS EPPERSON ST. DBLS: BROWN CRAWLER ST. DRIVER #1 ST. DRIVER #2 2-standins ATMOS 3-pedestrians	2-6/8	PROPS: A.J.'s gun Rick's gun Brown's gun Nixon's gun Jenkins' rifle VEHICLES: Dismantled pickup Power wagon Epperson's car St. Car #1 St. Car #2 SPEC. EFX: Radiator gag CAMERA: 2nd camera crew	D-1
	EXT. ROOFTOP/GARAGE POV Scs. 11A,13A Shooter readies himself to fire.	A.J. RICK BROWN NIXON JENKINS NIGHT CRAWLER 4-standins	4/8	PROPS: Hunting rifle w/3X to 9X scope MAKE-UP: Surgical tape on nose	D-1
	END OF 2ND DAY		TOTAL PAGES: 6-1/8		
3RD DAY WEDNESDAY 7/16/86 MOTION PICTURE HOME, CALABASAS NOTE: 2-CAMERAS	EXT. HOSPITAL Sc. 21 Establish.	ATMOS 2-nurses 1-male attendant 1-female patient 1-male patient 2-male doctors 1-female doctor 4-hospital visitors	1/8	PROPS: Wheelchair Crutches	D-2
	(3RD DAY CONTINUED)				

Figure 7-4. (continued).

```
                 SHOOTING CALL              FILM
             UNIVERSAL CITY STUDIOS, INC
      Due to Extreme Fire Hazard. Please Be Careful Smoking. Use Butt Cans.          Unit      4   Day of Shooting
```

Production STILL PHIL AFTER ALL THESE...	No. 62211	Director V. MCEVEETY

Series SIMON & SIMON - 1 HR.	Date MONDAY, 7/28/86

Art Director CRONE	Shooting Call Time 7:45AM	Condition Of Call R/S

Set Dresser DECINCES	[X] REPORT TO LOCATION	☐ BUS TO LOCATION

CREW CALL: 7AM.....REPORT TO LOS FELIZ. 16 MILES R/T.*REVISED

PAGES	SET DESCRIPTION	SC. NO.	D/N	LOCATION
5/8	EXT. HIGH SCHOOL (CECILIA,ELEANOR,ATMOS.)	4	D-1	JOHN MARSHALL,H.S. 3939 TRACY
2-1/8	EXT. H.S. LAWN-PANCAKE BRKFST. 36A,39 (AJ,RICK,CECILIA,WILLIAMS,BRIGHTON,ELEANOR, SHIRLEY,ATMOS.)		D-2	LOS FELIZ 213/660-1440
1-2/8	EXT. H.S. LAWN-PANCAKE BRKFST. 40 (AJ,RICK,CECILIANWILLIAMS,BRIGHTON,ELEANOR, SHIRLEY,ATMOS.)		D-2	
3-4/8	INT. H.S. UTILITY ROOM(TARP) 81,82PT,88 (AJ,RICK,DOWNTOWN,PHIL,WILLIAMS,BRIGHTON,ATMOS.)		N-3	

CAST AND BITS	CHARACTERS	RPT TO	CALL TIME	ON SET
JAMESON PARKER*	A.J. SIMON	PU@HOME	LOC@730A	815A
GERALD MCRANEY*	RICK SIMON	PU@HOME	LOC@730A	815A
MARY CARVER	CECILIA SIMON	PU@HOME@6A	615A	745A
TIM REID (NEW)	DOWNTOWN BROWN	W/N@1130A		
STUART WHITMAN	PHIL GAINES	W/N@1130A		
DENNIS PATRICK	CHUCK WILLIAMS	LOC	730A	815A
PAT CORLEY	DON BRIGHTON	LOC	730A	815A
NANCY KULP	SHIRLEY GRAHAM	LOC	645A	815A
PATRICIA BARRY	ELEANOR FINELY	LOC	615A	745A
BILL BURTON	UTILITY STUNT	HOLD		
* N.D. BREAKFAST PROVIDED				

ATMOSPHERE AND STANDINS	RPT TO	CALL TIME	ON SET
3 SI'S (BARTLETT,JEPSEN,MACE)	LOC	7A	
6 STUDENTS (3M,3W)WILL CHG. TO CHEFS & WAITERS & WAITRESSES-2 W/CARS	LOC	718A	
6 ADULTS (2M,4W)-TEACHERS,NEIGHBORS W/CHG. FOR PANCAKE BRKFST.-1 W/CAR	LOC	718A	
48 CLASS REUNIONERS (23M,25W)	LOC	8A	
1 SI (BALLARD) W/DRESS SDPD	LOC	2P	

************************** ADVANCE ********************************

```
TUE., 7/29:
INT. HIGH SCHOOL GYM-PARTY SC 78-80,89         N  JOHN MARSHALL H.S.
INT. GYM-TAG                SC 90-92           D  LOS FELIZ
INT. GYM                    SC 9,10            D

WED., 7/30:
EXT/INT. MUFFLER SHOP       SC 44-50           D  MIDAS MUFFLER SHOP
EXT. MUFFLER H.Q.           SC 51              D  LAUREL CYN. BLVD.
INT./EXT. POWER WGN.-TOW    SC 41-43           D  NR. OXNARD
```

RLL

SEE MAP 62211-25

FORM 2926 (REV. 7/83)

Figure 7–5a.   Shooting call for *Simon & Simon*.

PRODUCTION REQUIREMENTS

UNIVERSAL STUDIOS **FILM** Production **STILL PHIL AFTER ALL THESE...**

Director	Production No.	Shooting Time	Date
V. MCEVEETY	62211	7:45AM	MONDAY, 7/28/86

Set		Location	Phone
# 51 EXT./INT. HIGH SCHOOL		JOHN MARSHALL H.S.	213-660-1440
#		3939 TRACY	
#		LOS FELIZ	
#			
#			

No.	CAMERA		Time	No.	TECHNICAL		Time	No.	LOCATION		Time
	Cam:			1	Key Grip	BEAM	7A	X	Permits	AS REQ.	
2	Panavision	PKG	TRK	1	2nd Grip	SLEMMONS	648A	2	Police	MTRHOMES	715A
1	ARRI/BACKUP		TRK	3	Co Grips		7A		Firewarden		
	Zoom For:				Co Grips				Police/Cycles		
1	Dir. of Photog.	MARTINE.	7A	2	Crane Oper.	MURPHY	648A		**POLICE**		
2	Operator	CLARK+1	7A		Crane			1	Flag Person	CARS	6A
2	1st Assistant	MENONI+1	648A	1	Crab Dolly	HUSTLER	TRK		Set Watch		
1	2nd Assistant	NIZICH	648A	1		PEE WEE	TRK		Night Watch		
	Camera Mech.				Greens Person				Uniform Police		
	SOUND			1	CSE Setup		7A		Studio Firefighter		
1	Mixer	RIGGINS	7A		Painter				**HOSPITAL**		
1	Recorder	RODRIGU.	7A		Propmaker			1	1st Aid		7A
1	Boom Oper.	MITCHELL	7A	1	Special Effects	VANWEY	7A				
	Cable Person				Effects				**TRANSPORTATION**		Drv.
	Playbk. Oper.				Sing. Dr. Rm.			1	Driver Capt.	COORD	D 5A
	VTR Oper.							1	Co/Capt.	CAPT	D 5A
X	Booms	AS ORD	STG		Dbl. Dr. Rm.				Mini		
X	Mikes	"	TRK		Quad				Maxi		
X	RF Mikes	"	TRK						Sta. Wgn		
X	Mixer/Nagra	"	TRK		Schoolrm.			1	MAXI/PRD/WRD		D 612A
10	Walkie Talkie	PURDEPT	W/N	X	Heat Stg. #				Buses		
2	Megaphone	AS ORD	TRK		Heaters				Grip/Elec/Gen		
6	CHARGED BATTS.		TRK		**ELECTRICAL**			1	Duz All	460	D 6A
	SPECIAL PHOTOGRAPHY			1	Gaffer	HARMON	7A	1	Grip	359	D 6A
	Process DP			1	2nd Elect.	KENNEDY	7A	1	Elec.	357	D 6A
	Matte Supvr.			4	Lamp Opers.		7A	1	Generator		D 6A
	Matte Crew				Lamp Opers.			1	CAM/SND 360		D 6A
	Moviola & Oper.				Gen. Oper.				Prop		
	Grip				Generator			1D	San. Wgn 7 Rms.		6A
	Head Proj.				Wind Mach. Oper.			1D	San. Wgn 6 Rms.		6A
	Projectionist				Wind Mach.				Powder Trk.		
	Proj. Equip.				Battery Person						
					Batteries				Util. Trk.		
				1	Air Cond.	3PHS GEN	12N				
					Work Lights	FOR A/C		1	4 X 4	CC5412	D 518A
	STILL PHOTO			X	Wigs/Phone			1	MU TRLR		TOWED
	Still Photog.			1	40 PERSON		7A	1	Ward.		TOWED
	Still Eq. P/U				**PROPERTY**				Insert Car		
	FOOD SERVICE			2	Property Mstr.	ESCOBID.	7A		Car Carrier		
X	Caterer	MICHAEL.	6A	1	Asst. Prop	CHAVEZ	7A				
	Breakfasts				Benches For #			2	Jeep		TOWED
X	Walkng Breakfast	PER A.D.	W/N		Makeup Tables						
X	Gels Coffee X	Doz. Donuts	6A		Ward Racks				Water Wgn		
135	Lunches	20@1230P	1P	P X	Chairs	DIR/CAST	TRK				
	Dinners							1	Motor Hm. For		D W/N
	Suppers				**MAKEUP**				**PARKER**		
				1	Makeup Artist	DAWSON	6A	1	Motor Hm. For		D W/N
	UNIT MANAGER			1	Extra MU	WILSON	6A		MCRANEY		
1	Script Supvr.	LOOMIS	630A		Extra MU				Mechanic		
	Animal Handler				Body MU						
	Wrangler			1	Hairstylist	POST	6A		Pict. Equip.		
	Livestock				Extra Hair			1D	CECILIA'S CAR		530A
					Extra Hair				P/UP CARVER @		6A
	MUSIC				**COSTUME**						
	Piano Player			1	Mens Cstmr	JAMES/LV	630A				
	Music Rep				Extra Mens						
	Sideline Mus.			1	Ladies Cstmr	WING/LV	630A				

DEPARTMENT	MISCELLANEOUS & SPECIAL INSTRUCTIONS
ELECTRIC:	NOTE-3 PHASE GEN. FOR A/C-MUST HAVE 200AMPS PER LEG
ART/GRIP:	PRE-TARP GYM/PRE-TARP UTILITY ROOM
EFX.:	EXTRA E FANS

Assistant Director	Unit Mgr	Approved
VOGELSANG/MCKEE/+1	JIM GARDNER	BURT ASTOR

SEE MAP 62211-25

Form 2940 (Rev. 7/83)

Figure 7-5b. Technical requirements for one day's shooting of *Simon & Simon.*

Figure 7−6.   Jameson Parker (left) and Gerald McRaney (right) star as featured characters in the series _Simon & Simon._

Reshooting Requirements

Since a pilot film is crucial to the sale of a series, it is not uncommon for entire scenes to be reshot or amended during production. This occurs most often in action sequences, where the stunt is not as exciting as planned.

Scenes also might be reshot if the producer is not satisfied with the actor's performance or the director's work. In the pilot for _Knight Rider_, the ending sequence was reshot three times before the producer, Glen Larson, was satisfied. This sequence was important because it set up the relationship between Michael Knight and Devon Miles, and therefore the series premise.

While no one wants it to happen, actors sometimes are replaced during production. A child actor who read wonderfully in rehearsals suddenly cannot handle the stress on the set. An actress chosen for her appearance talks in a monotone and cannot remember her lines. The lead actor hates an important cast member, and the result is visible on the screen. Replacing an actor is always a difficult and costly decision.

THE POSTPRODUCTION PROCESS

Three steps must occur before a filmed pilot can be delivered to the network: rough assembly, director's cut, and rough cut. While the situa-

Figure 7-7.   Director checks script in preparation for shooting.

tion is analogous for tape production, for simplicity, this discussion deals exclusively with film processes.

Rough Assembly

While shooting is still in progress, the editors work on film already shot, cutting together sequences they show to the director and producer. If there is a question about a certain scene, everyone might gather in the editor's room to watch it on a Moviola.

Shortly after filming is completed, the editors assemble all the scenes sequentially and show the producer and director a first cut of the pilot. Length and style have not been considered in this compilation. It is simply a beginning point and contains a number of scenes that will not appear in the final version.

Director's Cut

By protocol and Directors Guild rules, the director is allowed to work directly with the editors to cut the film to conform to his or her vision of the project. During this phase, neither the producer nor network or studio executives are allowed to see the film.

Rough Cut

When the director has completed his or her cut, the film is turned over to the producer, who retains control until the pilot is delivered to the network. While maintaining some of the director's input, the producer usually recuts the film to suit his or her requirements.

At this point, time considerations begin to intrude. Currently, a two-hour television show contains ninety-four minutes of material (excluding an opening montage and end credits). An hour television show is forty-six minutes long. While a pilot does not have to be cut to exact broadcast length, it should be reasonably close. Films that are too long seem slow paced to audiences and network executives. If a film is too short, network executives worry about the sequences that are missing and must be included before broadcast. These are indications that there might be trouble with the film.

When the producer is satisfied that the cut is close to the proper length and in good shape, a screening is scheduled for studio or production executives. They watch the film, then make some suggestions. Sometimes these suggestions can be accomplished easily. At other times they require additional filming.

If the changes dictated by the studio or production executives are numerous, subsequent screenings of revised cuts might be necessary. Finally, there is a preliminary screening for network development executives who have been intimately involved in the project. Usually it is held at the studio. After the screening, the network executives offer their suggestions. The film is recut once again to accommodate these changes. The broadcast standards executives also attend this screening, and their suggestions must be accommodated before the film is accepted.

At this point, the film print itself looks as if it was left unraveled in the middle of a busy intersection. It has been cut and run through editing machines and projectors so often that it is worn out. The film negative remains untouched, however, and it will be used to make the final print.

The pilot subsequently proceeds through the final stages of post-production in rapid but usually uneventful stages. Music, sound effects, optical effects, replacement of unclear dialogue, and dubbing of the sound track follow. The completed show is finally ready for delivery to the network for consideration as a series. It will be delivered in one of two forms, depending on the wishes of the network and time considerations: an answer print or a dubbed rough cut.

If there is sufficient time, film editors cut the negative to form a final version, make a new print from the negative, and combine it with the completed sound track for delivery. This is known as an *answer print* and is a totally finished film.

More often, because of time considerations and because the pilot is not formatted to exact broadcast length, the film is not finished before delivery. A clean print is made from the negative, and a temporary sound track is compiled using music from records and old movies. This film, called a *dubbed rough cut*, is then delivered to the network.

Finally, the pilot is finished. The top network management team watches the pilot in a screening room. Sometimes the producer is allowed to attend this screening, sometimes not. After viewing the pilot, network executives rarely express an opinion about whether they will order the series or not. Many other factors must be considered before making that decision.

Network Decision-Making Strategies in Primetime Television: New and Current Series

III

1986-1987 PRIME TIME SCHEDULE

Day	Network	8:00-8:30	8:30-9:00	9:00-9:30	9:30-10:00	10:00-10:30	10:30-11:00
MONDAY	ABC	MacGyver		ABC Monday Night Movie			
	CBS	Kate & Allie	My Sister Sam	Newhart	Cavanaughs	Cagney & Lacey	
	NBC	A.L.F.	Amazing Stories	NBC Monday Night Movie			
TUESDAY	ABC	Who's the Boss?	Growing Pains	Moonlighting		Jack & Mike	
	CBS	Spies		CBS Tuesday Night Movie			
	NBC	Matlock		Hill Street Blues		T.B.A.	
WEDNESDAY	ABC	Perfect Strangers	Head of the Class	Dynasty		Hotel	
	CBS	New Mike Hammer		Magnum P.I.		Equalizer	
	NBC	Highway to Heaven		Gimme a Break	Tortellis	St. Elsewhere	
THURSDAY	ABC	Our World		Colbys		20/20	
	CBS	The Wizard		Simon & Simon		Knots Landing	
	NBC	Cosby Show	Family Ties	Cheers	Night Court	L.A. Law	
FRIDAY	ABC	Webster	Mr. Belvedere	Gung Ho	Dads	Starman	
	CBS	Scarecrow & Mrs. King		Dallas		Falcon Crest	
	NBC	Stingray		Miami Vice		Crime Story	
SATURDAY	ABC	Sidekicks	Sledgehammer!	Ohara		Spenser: For Hire	
	CBS	Outlaws		CBS Saturday Night Movie			
	NBC	Facts of Life	'227'	Golden Girls	Amen	Hunter	

Day	Network	7-7:30	7:30-8	8-8:30	8:30-9	9:00-9:30	9:00-9:30	10:00-10:30	10:30-11:00
SUNDAY	ABC	Disney Sunday Movie				ABC Sunday Night Movie			
	CBS	60 Minutes		Murder She Wrote	Designing Women	Nothing is Easy	Hard Copy		
	NBC	Our House		Easy St.	Valerie	NBC Sunday Night Movie			

8

Network Decision Factors: Testing and Scheduling

While the majority of network executives would like the world to believe that program decisions are made on the basis of gut feelings and showmanship, the reality is that there are two other major factors that influence whether a project becomes part of the network family of programs. These are audience research testing and scheduling practices.

AUDIENCE RESEARCH TESTING

While program executives tend to downplay the importance of research and even denigrate it as useless, misleading, and false, they cannot ignore it. Consequently, it does play an important role in the final selection of new shows.

Gathering Research Material

The networks gather research material on the shows by testing them before preview audiences. The sole function of special departments is to analyze the results and report the findings to the programming department and executive management. The testing itself is performed in three ways: group discussions, theater tests, and in-home testing via cable.

127

Group Discussions

Groups that view and discuss the film are called *focus groups*. They are selected by audience researchers in various cities, most often New York and Los Angeles. The groups are supposed to be representative of average television viewers in age, sex, and other demographic characteristics.

Typically, a group is invited into a conference room, where the participants watch a television pilot. Afterward, a moderator leads a discussion about the show, asking the group's opinions of the show's strengths and weaknesses and whether the group liked the concept and characters. These sessions are tape-recorded and frequently videotaped. After a number of such sessions, the research analyzers summarize the results and issue a report.

Theater Tests

Theater tests are conducted by ABC and NBC. CBS uses its own system developed by one of the network's longtime executives, Frank Stanton. The CBS technique combines theater test hardware with group discussions.

Most theater tests are performed by ASI Market Research, which operates a theater called Preview House in Los Angeles. Approximately 400 people are selected and invited to a special screening.* Once inside the theater, they fill out a demographic questionnaire. About 250 of the participants are asked to turn a dial while watching the program to indicate whether they are enjoying or not enjoying what they are viewing. This generates a minute-by-minute audience reaction chart.

Afterward, all the participants are asked to complete an extensive questionnaire detailing their attitudes toward the show, the concept, and the characters, as well as questions intended to measure the intrinsic strength of the program and their own viewing intentions for the possible series. Figure 8−1 shows typical excerpts from an ASI questionnaire.

Some of the closed-ended questions are measured against normative figures derived from years of program research at ASI. The first question measures the program's appeal: How much did you enjoy the program you have just seen? The second question provides a base for assessing viewing intentions: How interested would you be in seeing this weekly television program? A later question measures the effectiveness of pacing: How would you rate the pace? The open-ended questions offer the viewer a chance to discuss specific elements they liked or disliked.

─────────────────

*The respondents are selected by methods such as phone solicitation and shopping center surveys to represent national viewing tastes.

FOLDER #_____

PLEASE CIRCLE THE NUMBER NEXT TO YOUR RESPONSE TO EACH QUESTION.

And now... after seeing this television preview...

1. How much did you enjoy the program you have just seen? Please circle the number next to the ONE phrase that best describes your feeling.

    EXCELLENT - One of the best programs I've seen on TV...... 1   (16)

    VERY GOOD - Better than most TV programs I've seen........ 2

    GOOD   - About as good as most other TV programs....... 3

    FAIR   - Not as good as most other TV programs......... 4

    POOR   - One of the worst TV programs I've seen........ 5

2. Suppose the program you just saw became the basis for a one hour television series. Please tell us how interested you would be in seeing ISLAND SONS as a one hour weekly television program. (Circle ONE only.)

    Very interested.................. 1   (17)

    Mildly interested............... 2

    Not interested.................. 3

3. What did you like about ISLAND SONS? (Please be specific.)

_____

_____

_____

_____

4. What, if anything, did you dislike about the program? (Please be specific.)

_____

_____

_____

_____

(PLEASE TURN PAGE)

6/24/86

Figure 8-1. Sample pages from a typical ASI Market Research questionnaire.

FOLDER #_____

PLEASE CIRCLE THE NUMBER NEXT TO YOUR RESPONSE TO EACH QUESTION.

7. Please circle the number next to the words below that you feel best
   describe the program. (Circle as many as apply.)

Enjoyable................ 1	(36m)	Entertaining............. 1	(38m)
Realistic................ 2		Made me uncomfortable.... 2	
Corny.................... 3		Action-filled............ 3	
Relatable................ 4		Romantic................. 4	
Believable............... 5		Imaginative.............. 5	
Confusing................ 6		Boring................... 6	
Silly.................... 7		Humorous................. 7	
Different................ 8		Repetitious.............. 8	
Emotionally-involving.... 9		Exciting................. 9	
Ordinary................. 0		Dull..................... 0	
Predictable.............. 1	(37m)	Unbelievable............. 1	(39m)
For the whole family..... 2		Sophisticated............ 2	
Clever................... 3		Stupid................... 3	
Same old thing........... 4		Well-acted............... 4	
Fun to watch............. 5		Not my type of program... 5	

8. How would you rate the pace of the program you've just seen? Please
   circle the number next to the ONE statement that best describes your
   feeling.

   It moved too quickly............. 1   (40)
   It moved just right.............. 2
   It moved too slowly.............. 3

9. Please circle the number next to the words below that you feel best
   describe the character of Tim Farraday, the eldest brother who has the
   boat. (Circle as many as apply.)

Charming................. 1	(41m)	Warm..................... 1	(43m)
Brash.................... 2		Distant.................. 2	
Funny.................... 3		Sloppy................... 3	
Intelligent.............. 4		Casual................... 4	
Attractive............... 5		Phony.................... 5	
Competent................ 6		Hostile.................. 6	
Believable............... 7		Selfish.................. 7	
Too perfect.............. 8		Friendly................. 8	
Tough.................... 9		Likeable................. 9	
Compassionate............ 0		Cute..................... 0	
An interesting person.... 1	(42m)	Cold..................... 1	(44m)
Sincere.................. 2		Unsophisticated.......... 2	

(PLEASE TURN PAGE)

6/24/86

Figure 8-1.   (*continued*).

An adjective checklist is helpful in evaluating responses to the show and lead characters.

All this information, coupled with the audience viewing chart and focus discussion group, is used to evaluate the program's strengths and weaknesses. The data are compiled and analyzed by the network research staff, and a summary and report are issued for network management.

In-Home Testing

This technique was pioneered by NBC. Instead of a theater, where large groups of people must gather to view a program, the in-home technique uses cable systems around the country to transmit the pilot program on a special channel to selected groups of individuals. After being told the channel and time of broadcast, these households watch the program in their homes. Later they are telephoned and interviewed extensively. The interview is similar to the written questionnaire handed to participants in the theater tests. The interview material is codified, analyzed by the network research staff, and reported to network management.

The Accuracy of Research

The function of research in the selection process is highly controversial. It is disliked by the creative staff, who after spending nine months on a project and working closely with network programming executives, suddenly find their efforts judged by the cold, impersonal research process. Understandably, writers and producers are frustrated by the process, decrying the judgments made by "computers."

Network executives recognize that research is an unwelcome necessity mandated by the unusual nature of television. In most businesses, success or failure is easy to quantify. For a manufacturer it is sales. Demand for a product generates consumption, which results in high sales and a desire for more production. A poor or unnecessary product soon disappears because of lack of buyers. In theater or motion pictures, success or failure also is quickly evident: Either the theater is full, or it is empty.

These easy evaluations do not exist for network television. There is no contact between the manufacturer (the producer or studio), the distributor (the network), and the consumer (the viewer). To compensate for this, the Nielsen rating system was established to determine how many people watch a given show (whether the theater is empty or full). Since the networks are limited by the FCC to twenty-two hours of primetime programming, program research was developed to determine whether people liked or disliked what they were offered in this limited time.

The great difficulty with research stems from the fact that, while it might appear to be a science, it is in fact more of an art. Collecting the data is not difficult; analyzing the results and coming to valid conclusions are more complicated tasks. Much of this is because people are asked attitudinal questions, and in the case of television, they often lie about their opinions. This "lying" usually results from their giving either a social response or a hypocritical response.

Social Response

Sometimes people answer questions as they think they should, rather than honestly expressing their opinions. Most television viewers usually say they wish there were more quality programs, such as cultural events and documentaries, and criticize the amount of violence and number of silly shows that are on the air. Although they express these opinions, Nielsen computers show that, when offered a choice, people rarely watch the so-called quality shows.

Hypocritical Response

This is just the opposite of a social response. People often respond in interviews and questionnaires that a show is horrible if it contains sex or violence. They adamantly say they never watch such offerings on television. Yet Nielsen ratings show high viewing of violent and suggestive fare.

A good research analyst must be able to temper the numbers from the surveys with experience and judgment to draw valid conclusions about the test show. Overall, the research systems have proved to be much better negative than positive predictors. That is, they more often successfully predict failure than success. Since most television shows fail anyway, predicting failure also is a safer course. Still, the research departments must have a reasonable record of accuracy for the networks to continue to use them as much as they do.

A few years ago NBC's research department was engaged in testing the proposed fall series. One of the pilots was well done but basically disliked by network programming executives, who felt that it was slow moving and too sentimental. The research was so favorable, however, that they tentatively placed the show on their schedule. The show, *Highway to Heaven*, became a family favorite.

Another pilot being tested that year was well liked by programming executives but tested poorly with respondents. Viewers disliked the show's heavy use of violence and disruptive use of music. As a result, it almost did not make it on the fall schedule, but it finally was placed in a time slot where its failure would not substantially damage the network's ratings. Its title was *Miami Vice*.

Network programmers often find that using research properly is a difficult task. Ignoring research clearly is wrong, as no successful network programming executive can do without it. But using research as a crutch for every decision is equally wrong. Any programmer who allows research to override his or her better judgment ultimately will fail. Program research is a complex tool that requires much practice to use well.

SCHEDULING PRACTICES

Network scheduling considerations have a major effect on whether a project is chosen to proceed as a series. Scheduling theory is based on the principle of low entropy, an understanding that, despite the emergence of remote-control devices, the average viewer prefers to make as few choices (defined as channel changes) as possible. The result is viewing inertia, which allows networks to take advantage of audience flow (viewers tend to stay with a network's programming block unless they truly want to switch).

There is abundant evidence that the placement of shows can be as important as the shows themselves. Network heads of programming must be experts in scheduling. In their reigns as network programmers, Fred Silverman, Paul Klein, Harvey Shepard, and Michael Dann were considered superlative schedulers. In contemporary terms, Brandon Tartikoff at NBC is recognized as expert in scheduling strategy.

The effect of scheduling on the crucial decision of whether a pilot is accepted as a series is clear. If a program fills a need in the scheduling game plan, it is likely to be ordered, even if there are flaws in the show itself and the testing was not remarkable. Shows that are well liked by network programmers and that test well but do not fit scheduling needs often are passed over. A few of the better ones will be ordered as backup series, put into production to fill the slot of an early failure.

Of course, there are sensational shows that are so well liked that they are certain to become hits regardless of where they are placed in the network schedule. The problem is that these shows are as rare as white rhinos. Most television pilots fall into the gray area, where they show promise but are not guaranteed hits. Scheduling these shows becomes critical to the success or failure of the whole network lineup.

Scheduling Theories

Network scheduling theories fall into the following areas: target audiences, block programming, and counterprogramming.

Target Audiences

With the realization that the quality of the audience watching is as important as its size, networks recently have adopted strategies to reach key demographic groups. The bulk of the television audience remains over fifty years of age. This group is generally less desirable to advertisers, however, because they tend to purchase less. Advertisers pay a premium to reach younger people, usually with families, in the middle or upper-middle class, who have a significant disposable income. They also prefer people who live in urban areas rather than small towns.

While CBS has traditionally taken first place in the ratings race, ABC rose to prominence in the late seventies by capturing that highly desirable young audience. Their recent downfall can be ascribed to the loss of much of that audience to NBC, which has been successful in hitting this desirable demographic target.

Block Programming

In the effort to capture the target audience for the entire primetime programming period (8:00 P.M. to 11:00 P.M. in the Eastern and Pacific time zones), the networks rely on the concept of block programming. This entails scheduling compatible shows back-to-back for the entire three hours to take advantage of the principles of viewer entropy and audience flow.

Counterprogramming

Programming in blocks for the entire evening usually is impossible to achieve because of the appearance of at least one very strong, well-liked, highly rated show on a competing network. Recognizing that going head-to-head with such a strong show would be tantamount to committing suicide with any new series, the networks adopt the strategy of counterprogramming. This means scheduling a show that appeals to a target audience that differs from that committed to the dominant show.

The classic example of counterprogramming occurred a number of years ago when *All in the Family* became a megahit. There seemed to be no way to compete with this highly successful show. NBC turned to its research department, which discovered that the only audience not totally committed to *All in the Family* was children, especially boys, and some adult men. This fact initiated a search for a programming form that would appeal to boys and men. Someone thought of fire engines, and a show based on the exploits of firemen was conceived; it was called *Emergency*. While the show never beat *All in the Family* in the ratings, *Emergency* performed respectably for five years because it captured the audience not dedicated to *All in the Family*. ABC was unable to launch a successful program in that time period.

A similar situation existed on Thursday evenings at eight o'clock. *Magnum, P.I.* on CBS was the dominant show in the time period for a number of years until it was confronted in 1985 by *The Cosby Show*. While *Magnum, P.I.* dropped to second place, it still maintained a substantial following of faithful viewers. As a consequence, ABC faced the unenviable task of programming for a time period when there were virtually no uncommitted viewers.

Programming Concepts

Three other programming concepts frequently are employed in scheduling strategy. They are lead-ins, hammocks, and bridging.

Lead-Ins

The program preceding a specific show is called the lead-in program. It delivers its audience to the program that follows, much the way a relay runner hands the baton to his or her teammate. Obviously, programs that begin at eight o'clock do not have a network lead-in, except on Sunday, when programming begins at seven.

Eight o'clock programs are vital to a network schedule because they initiate network programming for the night. A strong eight o'clock show, such as *The Cosby Show*, can provide enough momentum for the network to dominate the entire evening's ratings.

The lead-in is particularly important for shows that begin on the half-hour (and are preceded by half-hour shows) and face one-hour shows on the competing networks. No audience can be counted on to switch in the middle of a show to view the second show in another network's hour block. Therefore, the maximum audience that the second show in a time block can receive is that delivered by the lead-in. Consequently, if the lead-in show fails, the show following it will almost certainly fail.

Hammocks

A hammock is a time period with strong shows preceding and following a particular program. A new show moved into a hammock slot is almost guaranteed a viewing audience. If the show is good or even acceptable, people will watch it. Failure of a show in a hammock indicates complete rejection, since the viewing audience must make the decision to leave the network for that period of time and then return when the next show starts.

Situation comedies, which often do not have a strong concept and rely on repeated viewing to build audience loyalty, fare best when placed in hammocks. Only very strong new comedies can stand by themselves. Usually new comedies are given a hammock position in their first year, and then, after becoming successful, they are moved to unprotected time periods, where they in turn provide a hammock for another new show.

Bridging

The term *bridging* refers to starting a competing show one-half hour before the competition. Prior to implementation of the prime time access rule, when network programming began at 7:30 P.M., networks scheduled a number of ninety-minute shows. Bridging was quite common at that time. With primetime reduced to three hours, however, the ninety-minute shows became unwieldy, and their ability to bridge the competition was reduced.

Today bridging is used most often on Sunday evenings, when the networks encourage afternoon sports events to run overtime, forcing them to push up the primetime programs. Thus *60 Minutes* quite often runs past eight o'clock, bridging the programming on ABC and NBC and delivering its large audience directly into *Murder, She Wrote.*

9

Current Programming

The pilot process and the creation of television movies and miniseries usually are considered the more glamorous areas of programming. Maintaining current series often is perceived as frustrating, tedious, and difficult work. Accordingly, current programming departments at the networks and studios often are staffed with burnt-out executives who have been relegated to the boneyard of current projects or youngsters just learning the business, hoping to gain experience and to obtain a job in development.

Despite its lack of glamour, current programming is vital to a network or studio and can spell the difference between success and failure. This chapter explores the function of the current programming department and its methodology and operations.

IMPORTANCE OF CURRENT PROGRAMMING

The critical function served by the current programming executives is defined by three parameters of the business as it exists today: the failure ratio, development costs, and syndication requirements.

The Failure Ratio

Despite the best efforts of network programmers and writer-producers, the failure ratio of new television series is enormous for many of the reasons discussed in previous chapters. Currently, only one out of ten new series is renewed beyond its original episode order (usually thirteen episodes). To exceed this 10 percent ratio is considered excellent. Often, as happened to NBC in 1983, a network will find that its entire fall slate of new series is rejected by the viewing audience.

If the failure ratio is too high over a sustained period of time, the lack of new series success, coupled with the gradual deterioration of established shows, bodes ill for the network as a whole. Recently, ABC learned this lesson all too well in its four-year fall from first to last place in the Nielsen ratings.

A high failure rate of new offerings places much of the network's hope for success in its ongoing series. Moreover, established series are the foundation and support for new series. A network's success is directly related to the number of highly rated shows it has and the maintenance of those shows. If a network has a number of well-received, well-viewed series, it can easily provide a large audience to sample new offerings, through both strategic scheduling and promotion. A faltering network with only a few well-liked series must place new shows in bad time periods without protection.

Despite the remote-control devices that allow viewers to switch channels from their chairs, audience research has shown that most viewers still have a nesting ground. This is the channel where they feel most comfortable and where they look first for their programming. If they dislike a particular program, they will look elsewhere for alternatives, but they will return to the home channel later. Different kinds of people have different nesting grounds. Older people and people who live outside urban areas have gravitated toward CBS affiliates. ABC used to have a hold on urban audiences, but that group has now moved to NBC.

If people become too dissatisfied with a network's programming, they migrate to a new nest. When this happens, the wasteland left behind is a third-place network, struggling to regain viewers. It is a very difficult struggle. They have lost their traditional viewer base and have only a remnant of viewers to whom they can promote their new shows. Executives at a third-place network are frustrated with the knowledge that they can schedule shows that probably would be successful on a rival network but will fail in their third-place environment. The converse also is true. More successful networks have shows on their schedules that are performing respectably but that would fail instantly in the rocky soil of network number three.

Development Costs

While each network tries to recoup much of its drama development cost by playing its long-form (ninety-minute or two-hour) pilots as television movies or specials, the advertising dollars received rarely meet the high development and pilot costs, and there is no substantive way to recoup the costs of passed-over half-hour or one-hour pilots. They are played as throw-away fillers in the network schedule. "Busted" pilots are shown during the summer months or during unimportant ratings periods such as the time around Christmas and New Year's.

As a rule, a network listens to approximately one thousand ideas per year, from which an average of one hundred projects proceed to script. Warren Littlefield, vice president of series programs at NBC Entertainment, said that for every ten ideas the network hears, only one script is ordered. For every five scripts ordered, only one usually makes it to pilot. He estimates that one of every three pilots eventually becomes a series, and that only two of every 10 new series return for a second season. This means that the ratio of ideas to shows that eventually make it to series is 150 to one, and the chances of having a hit with one of those ideas (that is, a series that returns for a second season) is 750 to one.*

With pilot writers receiving $30,000 or more, and pilot production costs topping $1.5 million per hour in drama and $900,000 for a half-hour comedy, the development tab for a network accumulates to an exorbitant figure. A successful network obviously requires less new development and therefore can be more selective and cost conscious. Thus, the rewards of high ratings are enhanced by lower development costs. A third-place network, however, must bear the brunt of its poor ratings and lower advertising revenue, along with considerably more development costs.

Experience has shown that no network can expect success if it replaces more than seven series in a season. The high development costs, coupled with the average success ratio, make mass replacement of shows hazardous in terms of both financial and audience success. Therefore, maintaining current series can have a substantial impact on a network's financial profile.

Syndication Requirements

For independent producers and studios, syndication revenues have been the "brass ring" on the merry-go-round and the principal financial impetus of television production. As explained in Chapter 7, studios and production companies produce network programming at a deficit; the cost of production exceeds the amount paid by the network for the

---

*"Searching for that 750-to-1 Shot," *Broadcasting*, 17 March 1986, 39.

show. The network licenses the show for two airings, after which all rights revert back to the production entity. If the show is successful and there are enough episodes, the production company can syndicate the series to stations across the country and around the world. After subtracting distribution fees and royalties and residuals, all the income is reimbursement to the company.

The amount of money earned by a successful syndication property can be enormous. *Magnum, P.I.* sold into syndication at approximately one million dollars per episode. With more than six year's worth of negatives, the earnings from a show like *Magnum, P.I.* can make a television operation very profitable and compensate for the losses sustained by aborted series and unsold pilots.

The crucial factors are numbers of episodes and success of the property. Of course, few unsuccessful series remain on the network schedule for more than one season. Generally it is calculated that a show must run for three seasons to accumulate enough negatives for a successful run in syndication. Interestingly, after ten years of network airing, the value of additional negatives declines, and the abundance of shows plus the long network run might actually hurt syndication sales. Facing this reality, a number of shows, such as *The Mary Tyler Moore Show* and *M*A*S*H*, decide to retire while syndication benefits remain high.

Figure 9–1. *Magnum, P.I.* sold into syndication at more than one million dollars per episode. Shown are Tom Selleck (right) and John Hillerman (left).

The value of syndication potential depends on the format and concept of the series. Situation comedies have been the best syndication properties. Their cost of production is lower than that for one-hour dramas, thus their deficits are low or nonexistent. Stations can play them during the morning, afternoon, early evening, and weekend, making them very desirable and profitable.

Eight o'clock action shows like *The A-Team* and *The Fall Guy* also are desirable for syndication. With their appeal to young people, they can be programmed in the afternoon and early evening hours. Serious drama shows are more difficult syndication sales. They can usually only be programmed by independent stations late at night (11 P.M. or after). Serials, such as *Dallas*, are even more chancy.

NETWORK AND STUDIO CURRENT PROGRAMMING DEPARTMENTS

The size and function of the staff dedicated to maintaining current programming operations vary considerably from the formally structured network operations to the frequently informal assignments within studios and production organizations.

At the network, current programming operations are major divisions of the programming departments. The head of the division carries a vice-presidential title, with subordinates designated as directors or managers. Each individual within the current programming department is assigned a number of shows. Five series is usually the maximum that any individual can handle well.

For every series, the current programming executive must read and comment on each script and view the rough cuts of all shows. He or she also is responsible for scheduling each episode by selecting the running order of those available. At the beginning of the season, half a dozen episodes might be ready to air, and the selection process can be crucial. By January the production schedule has taken its toll, and most series are existing hand-to-mouth. For the remainder of the season, shows are aired in the order they are filmed. Moreover, in most cases one-hour series have trouble meeting airdate schedules and require relief in the form of specials or the repeat broadcast of an episode.

Neither the production company nor the network wants to preempt a series very often. Ratings records clearly demonstrate that repeated interruptions of a series result in loss of audience. The absence of a series for just one week can cause a three- to four-point decline in audience share. If the period off the air is greater, the adverse effect is greater and the recovery time longer. The worst scenario is to have a show on one week, then off for two weeks, followed by a one-week airing and then a preemption. Only very strong shows can survive such a ragged broadcast pattern.

In studios or production companies, the role of executives in the current programming area is less formalized but generally more involved. The number of individuals working exclusively on maintaining current series varies from one individual to a staff almost the size of a network department. While studio or production executives might consult their network counterparts concerning the scheduling of series, their principal function is overseeing the production and story development processes.

Studio and production company executives are much more closely involved with the material than their network counterparts. They often participate in story development, read early drafts of the scripts, and view early versions of the episodes. They also might be influential in revising story lines, suggesting casting, commenting on the choice of director, and affecting the editing of completed episodes.

Studio and production executives also have the responsibility of controlling production costs. Conversely, if extra money is necessary for a desired stunt, if casting dollars are not sufficient, or if reshooting is necessary, the head of current programming has the ability to approve special expenditures. In most operations, the current programming executives also must approve all material, from script to finished film, before it is sent to a network.

EXECUTIVE CONCERNS: MAINTAINING CURRENT SERIES

The functions of current programming fall into three main areas: scripts, rough-cuts of episodes, and scheduling.

Scripts

While it has been amply demonstrated that series television is a character medium, where the presence or absence of a well-liked leading character can spell the difference between success and oblivion, no series can exist for any period of time without good scripts.

The common complaint voiced against almost every series focuses on stories. Poor scripts plague even very successful series. Virtually no dramatic series seems immune. *Miami Vice, Dynasty, Amazing Stories,* and *Murder, She Wrote* all have received story criticism.

Further, not all of this criticism is from television critics or the press. Within several months of the launching of any new series, the star usually begins to grumble about the quality of the scripts. What has occurred is that the actor, living with the role almost continuously, has become more of an expert on the series than the writers. As time progresses, the star demands more and more input into the script process, until he or she almost inevitably takes over the creative reins of the show. Sometimes this is a very successful collaboration, such as Alan Alda's involvement with *M*A*S*H* or Bill Cosby's control of his show. At other times it becomes destructive, such as Robert Blake's running of *Baretta*.

Everyone in television agrees that obtaining consistently high-quality scripts for episodic series is extremely difficult. There is a continual need for new writers and new material. Part of the difficulty is due to the limitations of such writing. The current programming executives make sure that each script qualifies in three major areas: series concept, presentation of the lead character(s), and story quality.

Series Concept

One principal question is asked by current programmers: Is the script faithful to the concept of the series? Too often, scripts veer sharply from the series concept. This happens for several reasons.

First, the writer and producers of the series grow tired of the show's format and want to do something different. While this occasionally is desirable, people watch a series every week because they like the concept and characters. Radically changing the concept is disruptive and can alienate viewers. Another common cause of concept deviation comes from new or outside writers, who find it easier to adapt the concept to their own ideas rather than working within the series' confines.

Deviating from the concept is most dangerous during the early, formative stages of a series. Often a producer or writer will want to produce an early episode that seriously deviates from the norm because it is a good script and can be aired later in the season. Invariably, other concept-conforming scripts have problems, and this unusual episode (perhaps focusing on a subsidiary character) ends up as the second or third episode on the air. Since this occurs during the period when viewers are still sampling the new shows, the results frequently are disastrous for the series.

In examining series scripts, it is important to recognize that a certain amount of predictability is desirable. People love to become familiar with a series and the habits of the lead characters. Who can forget that when Columbo finished an interview and reached the door, he would always turn and say, "Oh, just one more thing..." Everyone still remembers Jack Benny's classic reaction to being asked for money. And how about Jack Lord's famous utterance, "Book 'em, Danno."

Knowing the characters and how they behave makes viewers feel a part of the series. It provides them with special knowledge that the show's guest characters do not have. Viewers love this inside knowledge and rarely tire of seeing Higgens fume at Magnum, even though they know it is going to happen. In other words, it is welcome predictability.

Of course, predictability can be carried to an extreme with detrimental results. If the story is too predictable and each week's episode is the same as the last, the series becomes boring and the viewing audience tires of it just as they tire of a top 40 song. The solution seems to be a mix of predictable and unpredictable elements:

Predictable−Predictable = Dull

Unpredictable−Unpredictable = No Emotional Involvement

Predictable−Unpredictable = Just Right

Presentation of the Lead Characters

Protecting and properly servicing the lead characters are crucial to the success of a television series. Often in an attempt to be different or because of other concerns, the core characters are sacrificed for the sake of the story.

While it may seem obvious or terribly old-fashioned, it is important for lead characters to be heroes. They must face a significant problem, take charge of the crisis, and resolve it satisfactorily. Their actions must be the positive force that guides and resolves the crisis.

Interestingly, characters created as antiheroes have not worked on television. Antiheroes such as Jack Nicholson or Jon Voigt have become staples in motion pictures, but this type of character has not succeeded in episodic television. One might argue that Archie Bunker (*All in the Family*) was not a hero, but he was quite likable—in spite of himself—and the show revolved around the family of characters, not just Archie alone.

Thomas Magnum (*Magnum, P.I.*) might at first glance appear to be a weak hero, but this is not true. Don Bellisario, who created the character, is insistent that, while Magnum might be flustered and ineffective in comic situations or his confrontations with Higgens, this does not extend to his professional activities. If someone is in jeopardy, or if Magnum picks up a weapon, he is thoroughly proficient and definitely a hero. He gets the bad guy and helps those people in distress.

Researchers have explored this phenomenon of the hero in television and believe that it stems from the intimacy of the medium. The viewer is inviting the leading characters into his or her house. One of the strongest attributes used to distinguish successful from unsuccessful television characters is the question "Would you like to have (blank) as a friend?" We want our friends to be loyal, personable, and good. And that is how we want our television heroes to be, too.

In addition to behaving like a hero, it is crucial that the lead character resolves the crisis in the story. If outsiders (guest characters) solve the mystery or catch the bad guys, the hero is dispensable. It is important that the special abilities, insights, and skills of the lead character be responsible for the resolution. Thus, Perry Mason always won the case, Columbo always got the perpetrator, and Jessica Fletcher always solves the mystery. Once in a while, to keep the audience off balance, the lead character fails. But this is a once in a season, or a once in a series, occurrence.

Another major factor in portraying a lead character is providing insights into his or her makeup. Too often, a multidimensional portrait of a guest character is drawn at the expense of the lead. Series that make this mistake usually are short-lived because audiences find the continuing characters dull and one-dimensional. Successful, long-running series go to great lengths to explore the lead characters' attitudes, reactions, thought patterns, and feelings.

During the creation of a series, detailed biographies of the lead characters are developed and given to the writers. Too often, however, this biography is ignored or forgotten in actual production. Sometimes the writers and producers give limited information about the lead characters during the early part of a series, then reveal more as the show progresses. This can be effective, as long as the audience understands the thoughts and attitudes of the character at all times. The gradual unraveling then becomes a fascinating exploration of the lead, closely akin to the development of a relationship with a new friend.

Actors playing leading roles are particularly sensitive to this exploration of character. They find it critical for better viewer understanding of character motivations and actions. Understandably, actors push producers and writers to continue to explore the characters' many dimensions.

Story Quality

Every series receives criticism of story material. Writers become convenient targets of the network, critics, and performers. The writers themselves complain constantly about the difficulty of finding appropriate stories and developing good scripts. Many series writers feel that their program is the most difficult of any for which to write.

The fact is, writing for episodic television is an arduous and challenging task. New stories must be constructed to accomodate lead characters, and they must be told within specific series requirements. A good story has to satisfy viewer interest, star interest, and the producer's series parameters.

The parameters for writing a series are not unreasonable. In fact, they exemplify the basics of good drama: identifiable characters, strong conflicts, suitable adversaries, and satisfying resolutions. In addition, the series parameters require a faithfulness to the basic concept, which conveys a comfortable sense of predictability for viewers each week. In short, a program executive is concerned about satisfying these elements in episodic storytelling:

1. Giving the audience a reason to watch.
2. Having a strong and suitable conflict in the episode.
3. Providing worthy adversaries for the lead characters.
4. Sustaining faithfulness to the overall series concept.
5. Offering viewers the right amount of predictability.

Giving the Audience a Reason to Watch. Given the nature of television, it is possible for a good episode to get lost in the morass of other viewing material. It competes for attention with commercials, the promotion of weekly television movies and specials, independent stations and cable, and the clutter at the beginning and end of each program.

The networks try to maintain the visibility of a series through on-air promotion. To promote the shows effectively, however, they need what is called a *logline*, a reason to watch that is intriguing and salient, which can be placed in a print ad or used as the core of a thirty-second promo. A logline is a one-sentence description of the episode which catches viewers' attention and piques their curiosity. The word originates from its use in *TV Guide* listings. A good logline might be: "Fonzie goes blind, this week on *Happy Days*" or "Mark Harmon discovers he has AIDS on *St. Elsewhere*."

Some years ago, when *Happy Days* was the megahit of television, a teenager wrote a letter to the *Los Angeles Times* to complain about the show. He said it was pretty terrible, but he watched it every week. Why? To his frustration, he admitted that the on-air promotions were so inviting that they always made him watch. Ultimately, of course, such promotion loses its value if the show does not fulfill the expectations laid out in the logline. But many shows have been helped by the successful use of loglines.

Having a Suitable Conflict. Conflict is an essential element in both drama and comedy stories. An important part of maintaining any series is ensuring that there are suitable and sufficient sources of conflict within an episode.

A major source of conflict is the adversary, also known as the bad guy or heavy. The function of the adversary goes beyond providing a source of story conflict. In most stories, the adversary becomes the major antagonist facing the show's lead character. A common mistake in both drama and comedy shows is to make the adversary humorous or incompetent. Doing so often destroys the lead's credibility. If the adversary is weak, stupid, or incompetent, it does not take much of a hero to face and defeat him or her.

Providing Worthy Adversaries.   Even in adventure comedy programs, it is vital that the adversary be believable, powerful, and competent. Under the best circumstances, the adversary is an individual who cannot be stopped by traditional authority figures or ordinary people. He or she can be overcome only by the smarts of a Columbo, the dedication of a Sonny Crockett, the humanity of a Cagney or Lacey, the superhuman abilities of a robot car (KITT), or the awesome firepower of an Airwolf.

A common problem encountered in larger-than-life adventure programs is finding a suitable adversary. Who can best Superman or overcome James Bond? This has led to the creation of supervillains. Whether the audience accepts these figures or not can mean the difference between the success and failure of the program.

Sustaining Faithfulness to the Series Concept.   It would seem obvious that a series story should exploit the distinctiveness of the series concept. But in the need to provide diversified stories on a weekly basis, the core concept can be overlooked. Part of the maintenance of any series concerns the care and preservation of the concept. Therefore, a good *Knight Rider* should have an action finish in which the car can show its unique abilities; a good *Murder, She Wrote* should highlight Jessica Fletcher cleverly unveiling the solution, to the bafflement of others.

Offering the Right Amount of Predictability.   As previously discussed, a good series episode is a combination of predictable character elements and unpredictable story elements. An important function in maintaining a series is making sure a story is not predictable from beginning to end.

Very often writers in episodic television employ a technique known as the *third act twist*. This refers to a piece of information or an event that occurs about forty minutes into the program and unexpectedly changes the story. Most *Magnum, P.I.* episodes use this device to provide an element of surprise. One of the first episodes of the series concerned Nazi hunters. In the third act of the story, it was revealed that the kindly Jewish couple were in reality former Nazis. This turned the story inside-out, as the people who were supposed to be "good guys" became "bad guys," and vice versa.

The *monkey wrench* is another popular method of creating unpredictability. It comes into play when an unexpected event throws a careful plan into disarray. Usually the viewing audience is told of an elaborate plan. For example, the A-Team is going to break into the antagonist's fortress. The characters plan the attack so that they, and the audience, know the supposed sequence of events. The attack begins. But at a crucial point something goes wrong (the monkey wrench), and our heroes are trapped. What will happen? It is difficult not to stay tuned to the conclusion.

Rough Cuts of Episodes

The second major responsibility of current programming management concerns the viewing of the formative versions of series episodes. An episode of a television series normally progresses through the following editing steps:

1. Shortly after completion of filming, the director works with the film editor and assembles the film until he or she is satisfied with the results. The *director's cut* is then shown to the head producer of the series.
2. The producer evaluates the director's work and then makes whatever changes he or she feels are necessary. The producer must be more cognizant than the director of the proper formatting for the network (act lengths, station breaks, and so on) and the overall running length of the show. Currently, one-hour primetime shows run slightly longer than forty-six minutes. The producer might view various cuts of the show a number of times until he or she is satisfied.
3. The episode is then viewed by the current programming executives at the studio or production company. If changes are required, a discussion with the key producer follows. If the episode has severe problems, subsequent reedited versions will be screened until all parties are satisfied.
4. The episode is screened by the network's current programming executives. If they are dissatisfied, additional editing might be necessary. This is infrequent, however.
5. After final approval, the film negative is edited, and a final version of the show proceeds through the postproduction process, resulting in an *answer print* of the show.

Clarity

Because of modifications to the script or problems that surface in the filming, the assembled film often has moments that are confusing or illogical. The two most common methods of solving these problems are inserts and wild lines.

An *insert* can be defined as any shot or sequence of shots that does not use the actors and is not filmed with sound. Usually inserts are close-ups of objects, which are inserted after the principal photography is finished. For example, the hero reads a message left by the telephone.

For clarity the audience sees a close-up of the message. Almost always the hand holding the note is not that of the actor in the piece.

If a show is very troubled, complex _creative inserts_ might be necessary. Whole sequences might be constructed from inserts, such as the mysterious shots of feet walking into a room.

Wild lines are pieces of dialogue that actors did not say during the filming process. It is often possible for an attentive viewer to identify wild lines. If done improperly, the sound level of the wild line dialogue might differ slightly from its surroundings.

Most often, however, wild lines are identifiable from the editing style. When the camera is far back, so that the actor's mouth is not visible, any kind of dialogue can be substituted. A common use of wild lines are in automobile shots, where the actor's face and mouth cannot be seen. This provides the opportunity to add dialogue that was not originally scripted but helps clarify the story.

Another technique for increasing clarity is judicious editing. When the camera is on the back of someone's head, that character can say anything the producer wants. Trickier is the technique of cutting between two people having a conversation. If the shot on the screen is of one person listening to another character, the dialogue probably was added or modified after shooting was completed. Sometimes in a conversation between two people, the audience never sees either party open his or her mouth.

Performance

While series television relies primarily on its lead characters, each episode has a number of important roles cast specifically for that episode. If there is a problem with one of the key actors, the whole episode can suffer dramatically. To some extent, problems can be solved through judicious editing. Wild lines also can help. On some occasions, if the problem is severe enough, an actor's voice might be replaced by another actor's to produce a better result.

Production Values

Because of the rapid pace of episodic television production, problems with action sequences often develop. Sometimes stunts do not come off as anticipated, or locations must be changed at the last minute. It is the responsibility of the current programming executives, as well as the producers, to determine whether the results are satisfactory. Since time and cost are ever-present enemies in the production process, it is difficult to reshoot entire sequences, especially stunt sequences. Sometimes this is done, but only when alternatives have failed.

Production can be assisted by the combination of inserts and stock footage. Every series creates a library of sequences that can be repeated from show to show. These include the hero's car driving down the highway or an expensive helicopter shot of the city. In addition, studios file and catalog footage. Television shows have been set in Honolulu, New York, and New Orleans without the production crews ever setting foot in those cities.

It is also possible to buy special effects footage used in motion pictures. The scenes of destruction from *Earthquake* and the dam collapse in *Superman* have shown up in different forms on many television shows. The eerie full moon from *An American Werewolf in London* has become a television staple.

Scheduling

Scheduling falls principally into the hands of the network's current programming executives, although studio or production company executives often participate in the decisions. These decisions fall into four categories: normal scheduling problems, handling weak episodes, matching the competition, and sweeps.

Normal Scheduling Problems

Since production on most series begins during the early part of July, a number of episodes are available for broadcast during the fall. By January, however, the discrepancy between the shooting schedule and the broadcast schedule results in an ever-dwindling lead time. A one-hour episode usually requires seven working days of shooting, or nine calendar days. Consequently, after the first of the year, virtually every series is airing episodes in the order shot and is finding it very difficult even making the airdates.

The function of the current programming executive then shifts from selecting the order of episodes to monitoring the series' production status to determine when a series must be preempted because it will not be finished by the airdate.

Handling Weak Episodes

Within the normal production schedule (twenty-two episodes per season), there are bound to be several clinkers—episodes that started out well but were plagued by problems. Perhaps the star was ill that week, the choice of director was unfortunate, or the weather turned bad. Whenever possible, these episodes are put on the shelf and scheduled when they will do the least harm to the series as a whole. Normally executives try to schedule very good shows to kick off a new season. They try to play shows judged to be poor either around Christmas, when television viewing is low and people are busy with shopping and other holiday activities, or at the end of the season, when a show is firmly established and a bad episode or two will not harm continued viewing of the series the following season.

Matching the Competition

In the competitive world of network television, a current programming executive is constantly aware of the programs on the other networks. Accordingly, the programmer tries to set the most advantageous schedule for his or her show.

If the competition one week is going to be particularly weak—for example, if a strong competing series is to be preempted for a news documentary—it is incumbent upon the current programming executive to make sure a strong episode takes advantage of the situation. If the converse is true—for example, a blockbuster stunt is scheduled opposite a series—the programmer might choose to run a weak episode rather than waste a strong show against hopeless odds.

Sweeps

There are four crucial ratings periods (known as sweeps) during the year: November, February, May, and July. Since the networks do not schedule original programming in July, that period is important only to independent stations. The November and February sweeps, however, are very important to the networks. Consequently, they schedule special movies and miniseries during these periods, with each network trying to capture the largest possible audience. The series episodes scheduled during sweeps also are of critical importance. Episodes shot on location, with special promotable stunts or guest stars, are made especially for sweeps scheduling.

TOOLS AND TECHNIQUES FOR MAINTAINING A SERIES

The current programming departments at the networks and studios try in every way possible to increase the productive lifetime of a series. Some of the techniques available fall into three areas: audience research, new additions to the creative team or series content, and character progression.

Audience Research

At least once each year, usually in the spring while planning for the next season is underway, network and studio executives undertake research to determine viewer attitudes about a program. They might conduct their own research or use a market research firm.

Research is done in various cities around the country. In most cases, these surveys are a combination of telephone interviews and group discussions. The questionnaires often are extensive, and interviews can take up to an hour to administer. People are asked their attitudes about many elements of a series, including lead characters, stories, individual episodes, music, and pacing.

After compiling the results and analyzing the findings, the research firm (or program research department) provides a comprehensive report that covers four main areas:

1. An assessment of overall attitudes toward the series.
2. An evaluation of all the continuing characters in the show, detailing their strengths and weaknesses.
3. An overall assessment of the story material and an evaluation of key individual episodes.
4. Suggestions for changes in the upcoming season.

The program executive uses this information to formulate the most effective strategies for sustaining the series and characters in the new season.

New Additions to the Creative Team or Series Content

It is not unusual for the creative team to become jaded long before the audience. Accordingly, after a certain period, usually two years, burnout becomes prevalent. To maintain the necessary elements of predictability and unpredictability and to inject freshness in the series, it usually is necessary to make changes in the series both behind and in front of the cameras.

Not visible to the viewing audience is the addition of new writers to replace those who are tired of the series. These new writers offer a fresh perspective and often introduce new directions for stories.

Visible to viewers is the injection of new elements into the series. These elements usually take two forms. First, there might be changes in the locale or setting of the show. The characters might find a new house or office, or perhaps they buy a new car. These are modifications to the basic structure of the show, which can provide new story ideas and a renewed interest.

The second change entails adding new characters to the series. A new regular character provides the opportunity for fresh story ideas. When *The Rockford Files* began its network run, it had only two main characters, Jim Rockford and his father. By the end of the series, there were a half-dozen regular characters.

Character Progression

Another common method of maintaining freshness is character progression. With the exception of characters in soap operas, the characters in most series remain frozen in time and place. They tend neither to grow older nor to change. Since characters are the principal reason most viewers choose one television show over another, making radical changes to any of the continuing characters can be a risky business. A number of series have changed their characters for the worse, and the shows were canceled soon after.

Still, having the characters progress can be a challenging and creatively fulfilling event. Marriages and babies are common events in television series history; the latter has tended to be a successful event, while the former has not. When Valerie married her boyfriend, in *Rhoda*, the series was over. Similarly, the culmination of the romance on *Cheers* was disastrous to the ratings, and the characters separated again.

Another method of character progression is through a device known as an *arc*. Borrowing heavily from the soap opera format, the arc relies on progressive story changes throughout an entire season. For example, when Mark Harmon decided he wanted to leave *St. Elsewhere*, the producers devised a story that progressed over a number of weeks, culminating in his death from AIDS. This was a highly successful ploy that generated high ratings.

Arcs need not be confined to deaths or births. What is required is the planning, as early as possible (before the initiation of production), of changes that will occur over the course of the season's twenty-two episodes.

Arcs differ from serialized stories in that the story progression is not contiguous, and the episodes usually do not have cliff-hanging endings. Further, they are devised so that the series episodes do not have to be played in sequential order. This is critical for reruns, where it can be disadvantageous to be locked into a particular pattern.

SPECIAL CONSIDERATIONS: STUNTS AND SPIN-OFFS

Two other considerations are important to executives in charge of current programming. They are stunts and spinoffs.

Stunts

Maintaining awareness and recognition of series television programs is a constant problem. Promotions for series usually are lost in the clutter of commercials and station breaks, often taking a back seat to promotions for the late evening news. Miniseries, movies, and specials are at the forefront of network promotion.

If it is necessary for a series to attract special attention (and that is vital for almost every series on the air), the producers and current programming executives turn to stunts to gain that recognition. Generally, stunts fall into three categories: special events, guest casting, and crossovers.

Special Events

Births, deaths, and sudden changes in episodic format that command attention form the basis for special events. *M*A*S*H* did an unusual episode in which Hawkeye dreamed he had died. *Moonlighting* filmed a 1940s flashback episode in black and white. *Magnum, P.I.* did a special two-hour episode in which it was revealed he had a wife. *Knight Rider* began a season with a special episode where the car, KITT, was destroyed by a giant truck. Perhaps the most successful stunt was the shooting of J.R. in the last episode of the 1985 season of *Dallas*, creating a summer of speculation about "Who Shot J.R.?"

Guest Casting

Series often turn to special casting to attract attention during critical ratings periods. Casting of public figures, sports figures, movie stars, music performers, and other known personalities as special guest stars has proved to be an effective method of attracting attention. While it hardly needed additional attention, *The Cosby Show* recruited Danny Kaye for a special episode, and Boy George visited *The A-Team*. Gwen Verdon showed up as Magnum's mother, and Nancy Reagan has appeared on several shows to promote her special causes.

Crossovers

When characters from one series appear on another, it is called a *crossover*. Because of contractual issues, crossovers are almost always limited to shows owned by the same producing entity.

Crossovers can be quite effective but are difficult to achieve. Not only must the stars be amenable, but production schedules must be coordinated as well. Further, crossovers must take place on shows that appear on the same network. No network will give permission for one of its stars to make a guest appearance on a competing network's program.

A very successful crossover was made between *Magnum, P.I.* and *Simon & Simon*. Both shows were on CBS and were scheduled adjacent to one another. The special two-hour episode began in Hawaii, with Gerald McRaney and Jameson Parker guest starring on *Magnum, P.I.*, and it continued with Tom Selleck, John Hillerman, and others guest starring on *Simon & Simon*.

The most elaborate crossover was planned by Aaron Spelling and ABC to launch their new series, *The Colbys*. Over the course of half a season, new characters were introduced on *Dynasty* in preparation for the crossover. After *The Colbys* premiered, several characters from *Dynasty* visited that series.

Spin-offs

The premiere of *The Colbys* also involved another strategem, the spin-off. Perhaps the master of the spin-off was programmer Fred Silverman, who recognized the advantage of beginning a new series centered on an already familiar and well-liked character.

Maude began as a guest character on *All in the Family*. Laverne and Shirley were recurring characters on *Happy Days*, as was Robin Williams, portraying a weird character named Mork. Valerie Harper was a regular character on *The Mary Tyler Moore Show*, and characters from *Dallas* moved to *Knots Landing*.

Sometimes spin-off characters become the stars of their own shows only after the demise of the original series. Ed Asner went from the humorous *Mary Tyler Moore Show* to his own dramatic series *Lou Grant*. The character Trapper John jumped years from *M*A*S*H* to his dramatic medical series, *Trapper John*.

A spin-off is no guarantee of success, as the list of failed attempts is long. In addition, removing a well-liked character from an established series might irrevocably damage the host series.

Developing Other Projects for Primetime Television

A scene from the television film "The Day After," with Jason Robards and Jobeth Williams.

Miniseries, TV Movies, and Specials

Miniseries, TV movies, and specials fall into a program category of their own. Unlike series, which build up a loyal viewer following over the seasons, these projects are based on a single concept with high promotional value. The development process is the same, but network approval is based on the potential for a national advertising blitz. It is not unusual to find an advertising campaign planned before a miniseries is actually shot. In the following discussion, you will find some specific examples of advertising and promotional packages designed exclusively for network miniseries and television movies.

Television films can be divided into two categories based on their length: miniseries (dramatic epics of more than four hours) and TV movies (films of four hours or less).

MINISERIES

A miniseries usually deals with an epic sweep of history. Characters are engaged in dramatic conflicts over an extended period of time. The stories might be based on historical sagas, literary epics, or any other narrative blend of truth and fiction. Although the stories can be of epic proportions, the concepts must be translatable into one or two sentences for the most effective promotional possibilities.

Historical miniseries are set in exotic, global settings. "Peter the Great" was a legendary story offering a sweeping panorama of the Russian people and their times. It boasted an all-star cast and was filmed in the Soviet Union. "War and Remembrance" was planned as a thirty-hour miniseries shot on location in ten countries, with an estimated production budget of sixty million dollars. Other historical sagas include expansive miniseries such as "Winds of War," "Marco Polo," "Shogun," "Masada," and "Christopher Columbus."

"Winds of War"

Popular books about historically prominent events are prime resources for miniseries. "Winds of War," based on Herman Wouk's book, told the story of an American family in pre-World War II days. It was produced by Dan Curtis on a 206-day shooting schedule, with 962 pages of script written by Herman Wouk. The program aired as an 18-hour *ABC Novel for Television*, presented in seven parts. The public relations office of ABC prepared an extensive national campaign for "Winds of War," with viewer guides, glossy brochures, and large press packets containing synopses of each night's program and a biographical sketch of the stars (including Robert Mitchum, Ali McGraw, Jan-Michael Vincent, and John Houseman).

The advertising campaign designed for "Winds of War" is indicative of the type of promotional requirements necessary for successful exploitation of miniseries concepts. Grey Advertising prepared the photos and copy for *TV Guide* and magazine ads; ABC produced the on-air spots. The posters and artwork featured different styles, moods, and copy.

For the opening night, a full-page ad was prepared for *TV Guide* showing a proud family dressed in the styles of the thirties, leaning comfortably against their convertible. Two of the men are in uniform, and the copy reads: "A story of America in love and war. Of a time when a nation learned to hope. Of a family who followed their hearts through a storm swept world. And left their mark on history."

Each night, *TV Guide* featured a different ad. After the introduction to the family, the ads showed various events and characters from the film. These pictorial montages highlighted scenes from battles against head shots of characters now known to the viewing audience.

In addition to *TV Guide* advertising, ABC carefully orchestrated promotion of the miniseries in on-air spots and in newspapers and magazines through the release of informative press packets and brochures, which generated many discussions and articles about the series, the stars, the author, and the times. The network also supported a well-researched viewer's guide, discussing the themes and issues raised by the film, with resources for further investigation. It was put together by Cultural Information Service and distributed by local ABC stations to viewers around the country.

The promotional campaign was the backbone of viewer sampling of the miniseries, and it paid off in the ratings. For the entire eighteen hours, "Winds of War" averaged an outstanding 38.6 rating and an extremely high share of 53 (of all homes using television at the time, 53 percent were tuned to ABC).

"The Thorn Birds"

"The Thorn Birds," based on Colleen McCullough's novel, was produced by David Wolper, Edward Lewis, and Stan Margulies. It was a ten-hour miniseries shown over four consecutive nights. The film was about an Australian family spanning four decades. The content was expansive, but the concept could be boiled down into a thumbnail sketch for *TV Guide* and the press: "Set in the Australian outback from 1920 to 1962, a wealthy, embattled family witnesses the growing love between one of its members—a beautiful, sensitive granddaughter—and a troubled, ambitious priest, leading them both into a moral quagmire. Based on Colleen McCullough's bestseller."

The artwork, posters, and advertising gambits were carefully designed to exploit the theme. One poster (Figure 10-1) features Richard Chamberlain (the priest) and Rachel Ward (the young girl) embracing on a beach. Above them, the caption reads, "Love. Unattainable. Forbidden. Forever."

The press photos featured grainy close-ups of the two lovers, with a steamy quote from reviewers. Over a close-up of the lovers kissing (Figure 10-2) we see a quote from *Newsday*: "an audacious epic of sex, violence, vengeance, forbidden love, searing heat, and noble self-denial." Another picture has a quote from *Newsweek*: "steamy, sultry, sensuous." By this time, the miniseries was subtitled "America's Favorite Love Story." The concluding episode was publicized by a picture of a resigned Richard Chamberlain in his priest's garb and Rachel Ward sadly facing away from him.

ABC also provided an extensive press packet for this series. It included a synopsis of each segment, interviews with stars Richard Chamberlain and Barbara Stanwyck, and background information on the entire cast and key production personnel. The stories and interviews were ripe for press coverage nationwide. A viewer's guide discussed the film in terms of social issues and constraints on women in society, with appropriate biographical resources.

Once again, the promotional campaign paid off handsomely in the ratings. The ten-hour miniseries averaged a powerful 41.9 rating and an extraordinary 59 share of the viewing audience.

Figure 10-1. Advertisement for *ABC Novel for Television* "The Thorn Birds," a David L. Wolper/Stan Margulies, Edward Lewis production, in association with Warner Brothers Television, © 1983 Warner Brothers, Inc. All rights reserved.

Figure 10–2.   Press advertisement for "The Thorn Birds."

"V" and "Amerika"

Although many miniseries are based on best-selling books, original fiction also can be a bountiful resource. The miniseries "V" was a science fiction epic set in the future, with a die-hard group of survivors battling earth's conquerors. The success of the multipart film spawned another version of the series, which captured viewers' imaginations.

Similarly, the miniseries "Amerika" was originally written for television and planned as a sixteen-part miniseries for ABC, depicting life in the United States after a takeover by the Soviets. In the development stages, with budgets still being written and cutbacks planned in many of the episodes, the project received enormous publicity. In 1986, the Soviets formally complained about Hollywood's portrayal of Soviets in films such as *Rambo* and *Rocky IV*, and they said the miniseries would adversely affect gains made in U.S./Soviet relations at the Geneva conference. Going one step further, they implied that if "Amerika" were produced, Moscow's ABC News bureau would be affected. Brandon Stoddard, ABC entertainment president, now had to contend with the political ramifications of capitulating to foreign pressure or, alternatively, appearing insensitive to the program's impact on viewers.

Thus the network found itself in a tumultuous situation concerning a miniseries that was not yet in production. "Amerika" was a highly promotable concept, threatened by cancellation while still on the drawing boards—and that fact increased public interest in and awareness of the project. What programmer could pass up that expanding global market? After intensive debate, ABC finally ordered a cutback to twelve hours and gave the go-ahead to producer Donald Wrye. In late 1986, the project was again restructured, this time as a fourteen–hour miniseries, with a grueling postproduction schedule to meet the proposed air date. That airdate (February, 1987) coincided with Nielsen's ratings sweep week. A month before the scheduled date, Stoddard revealed to a group of television writers: "We are now editing like mad. We have thirty editors working on this film. They're in eleven teams . . . We are in more danger on the postproduction of "Amerika" than any other show that I've ever worked on in order to try to make this air date."[*]

At the same time, Stoddard told producer Donald Wrye that he would permit the miniseries to be pulled from the February sweeps if the postproduction schedule proved insurmountable.

---

[*]"'Amerika' Falls Behind," *Variety*, 14 January 1987, 164.

TELEVISION MOVIES

Popular Books and Original Stories

All television films must have a promotable concept that can stand on its own as a major event in national newspaper and magazine advertising. As we have seen, popular books are a gold mine for miniseries development. Networks can exploit the promotional tenor of the book, which already has proven appeal.

"Roots" was based on Alex Haley's search for his own roots in black culture; it became the progenitor of an epic miniseries. "Fatal Vision," a four-hour television film, was based on the book about the Green Beret doctor found guilty of murdering his wife and family. The book piqued the public's imagination, and viewers wanted to know more about the crime, the suspects, and the investigation. That film was shown on two successive nights and became the top-rated primetime television film of 1985. Among other successful four-hour films are "Murder in Texas," "Dress Gray," and "World War III."

Quality fiction, however, does not necessarily mean high ratings. Ratings for the adaptation of Ernest Hemingway's *The Sun Also Rises* ranked among the lowest for any miniseries or television film in the 1985 season it aired.

Some original stories also are written for television films. Many exploit the promise of romance, love triangles, and sexual promiscuity. Television films with glittery titles such as "Sins," "Lace," "Harem," "Hollywood Wives," "Malibu," and "Club Med" featured characters and settings designed to exploit sex appeal.

Headline Events

Many original films are based on headline events and national concerns. These productions tap into emotional and political issues that affect public consciousness. "Do You Remember Love" starred Joanne Woodward in a gripping story about Alzheimer's disease. "An Early Frost" was the first television movie about AIDS. "Hostage Flight" dealt with the trauma of a terrorist hijacking. "The Burning Bed" dealt with the story of an abused woman who murdered her husband; it sparked national interest in problems of wife abuse. Another television film, "Adam," dealt with the problem of kidnapped children; it spearheaded a national effort to help find missing children through a national crisis center.

Another project based on real people and events was "Samaritan," the story of Mitch Snyder, an activist for the homeless in Washington, D.C. After a well-publicized hunger strike, Snyder received promises from President Ronald Reagan that the city's dismal shelter would be turned into a model facility, but the government later went back on its word. Producers Deborah Levine and Debbie Robins saw the plight of Snyder on CBS's *60 Minutes* and interested Charles Fries in helping negotiate the rights to the story. The deal called for Washington homeless to be hired as extras in the film and for profits to be shared with Snyder's center for creative nonviolence.

"The Day After"

"The Day After," a fictional account of a nuclear strike on Kansas City, is interesting to examine from the standpoint of its conception, production, promotion, and impact. The project began with a bold request from ABC to writer Edward Hume, inviting him to create a dramatic television film on the topic of nuclear war. Hume approached the assignment with great care, using six months for research before starting the script. Brandon Stoddard, then president of ABC Circle Films, and Stu Samuels, vice president for motion pictures, also discussed the project with producer Robert Papazian, who committed himself to the enormous task of developing and producing this controversial film.

Three years later, in late 1983, "The Day After" was finally ready for broadcast. The film, starring Jason Robards, Jobeth Williams, Steven Guttenberg, John Cullum, and John Lithgow, lasted two hours and fifteen minutes. Its synopsis for *TV Guide* was straight and to the point: "A drama about the unthinkable catastrophic consequence of a superpower nuclear confrontation as it affects average American citizens in the Midwest."

Brandon Stoddard was quoted in an ABC press release about his reasons for developing and airing this television film:

> We have lived for nearly four decades with the terrifying threat of an apocalyptic nuclear war and have all wondered what would happen to us if it were ever to occur. This film will provide an unrelenting and detailed view of a nuclear attack on the United States and what the effects might be on average citizens living in Kansas, far removed from political origins or explanations. It is our hope that "The Day After" will inspire the nations of this earth, their people, and their leaders, to find the means to avert the fateful day.*

---

*"The Day After" Press Kit, ABC Public Relations, New York, 20 November 1983, p.1.

The promotion was handled in an appropriately serious fashion, generating extraordinary interest in the television event. A poster (Figure 10–3) was designed to provide a concise sense of what it would be like before, during, and after a nuclear disaster in the Midwest. Four pictures filled the poster. The first showed a woman and her children in front of their home: "Thursday...The Day Before." The next panel showed a woman in front of her house looking into the sky, missiles flying behind her: "Friday...The Day Of." In the third panel, a reverse black-and-white negative of the house and trees, no one was shown: "Saturday..." The last panel was darkened, with just the copy visible: "This is what it would be like, if you were there that day, and...THE DAY AFTER. Beyond Imagining."

ABC News also announced that it would prepare a one-hour special edition of *Viewpoint* to be broadcast immediately after the television film. The news tie-in would allow experts to discuss the various issues raised by the film.

A press kit for the nation's newspapers and magazines provided background on the film, the creators behind it, and a list of pertinent resources on the issue. In addition, a viewer's guide was put together by Cultural Information Service, an independent nonprofit educational organization, with ABC supporting research, development, and distribution of the guide to local affiliates, schools, libraries, and the community. The guide raised provocative questions, offered interactive exercises to help viewers deal with the subject, and provided a selected bibliography.

"The Day After" was produced in a starkly realistic style, promoted in a focused and intelligent manner, and watched by an astonishing number of viewers. In its first showing in the United States, it garnered a 46 rating and a 62 share. It was the source of international debate and policy reviews at the highest levels of government.

Special Considerations

If a project is based on real people and events, the producers and network must be sure that appropriate rights have been obtained. While consent from the people depicted is mandatory, the legal considerations are complex, conflicting, and often unclear.

People depicted in docudramas generally are covered by a *right of publicity*, which requires consent before any name or likeness can be portrayed on screen. Conflicting interpretations of the right of publicity have emerged in different states, which adds to the problem. To minimize risks, entertainment attorneys seek appropriate literary and estate rights, and they recommend disclaimers about portrayals of characters and events on the screen.

Figure 10–3.   Poster advertising "The Day After."

SPECIALS

In contrast to television films or miniseries with highly dramatic subject matter, television specials are designed to be light and entertaining. They are either one-shots or perennials (shows that are produced annually). Perennial concepts are most attractive for networks and sponsors, since they build familiarity and anticipation from year to year. If we analyze the types of specials produced, they seem to fall into several categories: sports specials, holiday specials, awards shows, packaged events, "upscale" specials, and news specials.

Sports Specials

Sports events come at predictable times each year, drawing large audiences, particularly men. Among the yearly sports specials are the Super Bowl (which ranks among the top primetime specials), the World Series, NFL football, the NCAA basketball championship series, the Rose Bowl, the National and American League baseball championship series, Pro Bowl, the NBA basketball championship series, the Major League All-Star Game, and the Olympic Games.

These are specials in the sense that regular programming is preempted to make room for them. Unlike regular sporting events seen throughout the year, these represent highlights of each sport's seasonal competition.

Holiday Specials

Holiday specials are centered on the theme of a particular holiday season. Networks particularly like the perennial aspect of holiday specials, which can be produced in any form, from variety shows to animation specials. Examples are plentiful: "I Love the Chipmunks Valentine Special," "It's the Great Pumpkin, Charlie Brown," "A Charlie Brown Thanksgiving," "The Bugs Bunny Thanksgiving Diet," "Frosty the Snowman," "Dr. Seuss: How the Grinch Stole Christmas," "Bob Hope's Christmas Special," "Perry Como's Christmas Special," "Christmas in Washington." And the list goes on. Networks see these specials as being appropriate for family viewing during various holiday seasons.

Awards Shows

If it is a celebrity awards show, it probably will be covered by the networks. Throw in some live entertainment and big-name celebrity hosts, and the show will approach annual status. The most prominent awards shows include the Academy Awards (motion picture achievement) and the Emmy Awards (television achievement). Many other specials have been spawned in this category. Among them are the Tony Awards, the American Music Awards, the Grammy Awards, the People's Choice Awards, the Academy of Country Music Awards, and the Country Music Association Awards. Shows in this category rely heavily on star appeal—onstage, in the audience, and in live performances.

Packaged Events

A great number of specials fall into this catchall category. These are programs that are prepackaged with specific entertainers attached or other entertainment hooks to hold audience interest and bolster promotional value. Packaged shows can take several forms: celebrity causes and tributes, real events that are taped, and specially produced or packaged events.

Celebrity Causes and Tributes

Sometimes, prepackaged specials center on a celebrity cause. One legendary event was the "USA for Africa" special. It attracted top stars in every category of popular music and had a tremendous impact on world consciousness about hunger in Africa. The show raised many millions of dollars for relief efforts on that continent. A similar special was put together by Willie Nelson, Bob Dylan, and others to publicize the plight of farmers in the United States. Another program featured major entertainers in support of AIDS research.

Tributes are somewhat different. These shows are set up as tributes to a particular person for his or her achievement. Consider specials such as "Martin Luther King Special," "Bob Hope's Birthday Gala," "George Burns Birthday Tribute," "Dean Martin's Celebrity Roast "(usually with Red Buttons and other celebrity guests), "All-Star Party for Lucille Ball," "Johnny Carson's Anniversary Show," "Disneyland Anniversary Celebration," "Dick Clark's American Bandstand Anniversary," "Television Academy Hall of Fame," "Kennedy Center Honors," and "A.F.I. Tributes."

Real Events

Some packaged shows provide viewers with coverage of an ongoing event they might otherwise miss. These include "The Barnum & Bailey Circus," "The Magic of David Copperfield," and "Motown Returns to the Apollo."

Also in this category are the traditional beauty pageants. These specials feature people (usually women) in competition with each other. Among specials in this vein are the "Miss America Pageant," the "Miss USA Pageant," "Miss Teen USA," "Miss Hollywood," and "America's Junior Miss." Although women's groups object to what they see as the exploitation of women in these pageants, the networks continue to air them, as they draw sizable audiences.

Specially Produced or Packaged Events

This category is filled with show ideas, which run the gamut from journalistic interviews ("Barbara Walters Special") to filmed specials ("The Ewok Adventure"). The producer can make anything an event, including coverage of stars appearing in new locales ("Ann Murray: The Sounds of London").

Some producers specialize in developing and producing events that capitalize on contrived competitions, such as "Battle of the Network Stars," "Circus of the Stars," and "The College Cheerleading Championships." It is not much of a jump to even lighter entertainment fare, including "Life's Most Embarrassing Moments," "All-Time Greatest TV Censored Bloopers," and "The World's Funniest Commercial Goofs."

Specials are developed from a variety of sources, including independent producers who want to cover an event with big stars attached; theatrical agencies that package their own clients into major events; and large advertising agencies that seek appropriate projects for their clients. Some of the larger advertising agencies include Ogilvy & Mather, J. Walter Thompson, and Benton & Bowles. These agencies have specific directives from their clients to find appropriate television vehicles for their prescribed advertising budgets.

As an example, Texaco tells its agency that it wants to sponsor Bob Hope specials each year. Consequently, a diversity of Bob Hope specials are packaged and produced annually. In one year alone, 1985, the network aired "Bob Hope's Comedy Salute to the Soaps," "Bob Hope's Christmas," "Bob Hope Lampoons Television," "Bob Hope's Birthday Gala," and "Bob Hope Presents Unrehearsed Antics of the Stars." Never underestimate the power of a client-furnished package to the network.

"Upscale" Specials

While light entertainment specials are designed specifically to boost ratings, more upscale projects are not necessarily intended to be ratings contenders. Their main purpose is to build a stronger public image. A model of this "soft" programming approach is "The Kennedy Center Honors," a special taped in Washington, D.C., with an array of well-known entertainers and political spectators, including the President of the United States. Despite big names, the show annually winds up at the bottom of the Nielsen ratings. Still, it receives critical acclaim and the support of the network and sponsors.

Similarly, high-quality projects are not designed for high ratings but for image making. Dramatic specials such as "Death of a Salesman" with Dustin Hoffman offer a sense of respectability that lasts long after the broadcast. Some corporations are particularly receptive to enhancing their public image with upscale programming. Among them are Hallmark, IBM, Xerox, and Mobil. Programs such as *Hallmark Hall of Fame* and *IBM Presents* consistently generate a sense of quality programming among networks, sponsors, and viewers.

News Specials

News specials focus on immediate, topical events. Live coverage of headline issues, political speeches, and major national events is presented to the nation. These specials range from presidential news conferences to international crises covered live via satellite.

In contrast to the immediate nature of news specials, a magazine format explores more investigative stories and more informational topics. Various segments are produced as individual story units within the program. By far the most successful informational program is *60 Minutes*. Others have included *20/20*, *1986*, and *West 57th*. These programs are generated, produced, and guided under the aegis of the network news department.

The Pragmatic Side
of Primetime Television

Figure 11−1. One of the greatest areas of concern for broadcast standards executives is the portrayal of violence.

Constraints on Creativity

As you may have surmised, creativity in television is not unharnessed. There are many constraints on the creative process. Among the more common are self-censorship, government regulations, and political pressure groups.

In recent years, the Federal Communications Commission (FCC) has reduced its watchdog role over television programming, but it has been replaced by many public and private entities. Some of these groups maintain a constant vigil over stations that are granted lucrative licenses to broadcast over the public airways.

The core concern of censorship in television revolves around the questions of taste and control. The issue of taste can be traced back to the thirties, when the outcry about risqué material being shown in neighborhood movie theaters led to the creation of the Hays Commission to inspect and certify each film as suitable for consumption by all ages.* Of course, in those times daring programs featured the partial exposure of a breast or the beginning of an open-mouthed kiss before a fade-out. It was considered shocking when Clark Gable uttered, "Frankly, my dear, I don't give a damn" in *Gone with the Wind*.

---

*For more on the Hays Commission, see Arthur Knight, *The Liveliest Art: A Panoramic History of the Movies* (New York: MacMillan, 1957), 112–16, 239, 308; Thomas Bohn and Richard Stromgren, *Light and Shadows: A History of Motion Pictures* (New York: Alfred Publishing, 1975), 181–82. For more on federal and private control of television, see Erik Barnouw, *Tube of Plenty: The Evolution of American Television* (New York: Oxford University Press, 1982); Lawrence Lichty and Malachi Topping, *American Broadcasting: A Source Book on the History of Radio and Television* (New York: Hastings House, 1975); Charles Clift III, and Archie Greer, eds., *Broadcasting Programming: The Current Perspective* (Washington, D.C.: University Press of America, annual).

The issue of control in television derives from its accessibility to all households with enough money to buy a television set (and that is about 99 percent of all the homes in the United States). Much of the concern centers on the impact of programming on children. While there have been numerous studies of television's effect on children, the relationship is difficult to isolate with reasonable statistical assurance.

Unfortunately, the underlying assumption by most of those concerned about children being exposed to potentially harmful material is that the individuals watching television are unable to make intelligent program choices and are incapable of monitoring and controlling the viewing selection of other family members. The only acceptable solution, therefore, seems to be to eliminate those programs or program elements that might be deemed undesirable or offensive.

This attitude persists at the networks, despite the intrusion of cable and pay television, where many of the things banned on commercial television are available in abundance at all hours of the day and night. The rationalization is that the viewer purchases a cable service and therefore can decide whether to have "undesirable" programming in his or her home.

Recently a number of non-network stations have begun broadcasting uncut R-rated movies with a parental advisory notice at the beginning of the program. Little criticism of this practice has arisen, primarily because the movies selected have been award-winning classics. It is doubtful that stations could broadcast less prestigious material without substantial criticism.

The control of network television program content comes in two forms: internal reports from the network's broadcast standards department and public-interest groups that exert pressure on the networks.

BROADCAST STANDARDS AND PRACTICES

The television equivalent of the motion picture coding system is each network's broadcast standards and practices department, which monitors and controls the content of all material, including advertising and programming. The head of this department reports directly to the president of the network, at a level equal to that of the head of programming.

The central issue between creators and censors concerns the standards that are used in decisionmaking. The guidelines often seem arbitrary, leading to frustration among the creative people and hostility on the part of network standards executives.

For example, a few years ago there was a major dispute over an episode of *Simon & Simon*, in which victims were murdered by means employed in a novel. One of the victims was playing in a swimming pool with other people when she was grabbed underwater by the killer and handcuffed to the drain. The CBS standards executives deemed the sequence unacceptable because (1) someone might actually try to kill a person that way (replication) and (2) it was too graphic (the victim was shown being handcuffed to the drain). After much argument, the question of replication was dismissed as improbable if not impossible. The graphic nature of the crime was resolved by ending the sequence earlier. Instead of seeing the victim's wrist being encircled by the handcuff, the film was cut just as the handcuff began to encircle the wrist, a rather fine distinction between acceptable and unacceptable material.

At NBC and ABC the departments assigned to monitoring and approving program content are called _broadcast standards_. At CBS the department is named _compliances and practices_. While the names are different, the operation is the same. It focuses on five general areas: violence, replication, sex, language, and early evening program concerns.

Violence

Perhaps the greatest area of concern for standards executives is the portrayal of violence. ABC uses a counting system, permitting a certain number of acts of violence per show, depending on the hour of broadcast. CBS and NBC spurn counts but judge each act of violence independently for its severity and inherent relationship to the plot.

The intent is to limit superfluous violence while maintaining the integrity of the dramatic piece. Unfortunately, this often becomes confused by definitions of what is considered violent. For example, the slapstick act of squirting a seltzer bottle in someone's face or throwing food is given the same weight as shooting someone with a gun. Even more surprising, verbal threats often are counted as violent acts, but destruction of property is not. As a consequence, few television characters vocalize their anger with statements like "I'm going to kill you and spread your guts over the living room," but there are seemingly endless car chase sequences in which trash cans fall like bowling pins and cars flip and smash in ballets of destruction. To avoid the censor's wrath, people almost always escape from these spectacular crashes unscathed, a real piece of fiction.

Certain violent acts are considered especially reprehensible. These include shattering glass, people being consumed by fire, the placement of a weapon at a victim's head, and showing the impact of a bullet on the victim's body.

Replication

One of the earliest movies made for television was a Rod Serling story called "Doomsday Flight." It involved threatening an airline by placing a bomb in a piece of baggage. If the plane tried to land before the ransom was paid, the bomb would explode. In the film it was discovered that the bomb was triggered by any altitude lower than five thousand feet. The problem was solved by landing the plane in mile-high Denver. Shortly after the movie aired on network television, a real airline received the same threat as the one portrayed in the movie. Programmers and network executives quickly became aware of the danger of exposing potentially dangerous ideas to the public.

This was followed by the famous "Born Innocent" incident in which the rape of a young woman in prison was followed a few weeks later by the same event in real life. As a direct consequence, there is now strict supervision of scripts to prevent a casual television viewer from learning a particular criminal activity. Even a commonplace event such as a private detective picking a door lock is never shown in detail and is made to look far easier than it is. When a procedure is carefully explained and demonstrated, it is almost always incomplete and inaccurate. For example, in the pilot episode for *The Insiders*, one of the lead characters was taught how to break into a car and hot-wire it. The sequence raised a furor among network executives, until it was explained that there were deliberate errors in what was shown and that no one could successfully steal a car replicating those procedures.

Sex

If violence occupies center stage in the life of a broadcast standards executive, sex stands just slightly behind in second position. This is one area where the rules of acceptance and rejection are clear and rarely in dispute. While bare breasts might be common in motion pictures and cable programs, they remain unacceptable on network television.

Writer/producer Roy Huggins likes to recount an amusing incident that occurred a few years ago concerning a miniseries he produced for NBC. Care was taken in a bedroom scene to ensure that, while the actress was bare breasted, the bottom of the television screen would not reveal more than the acceptable top of her bosoms. When the film was completed, it was screened for the network and approved by the standards department. What no one realized was that the frame size projected in the screening room was slightly smaller than what would be used in the actual telecast. When Huggins turned on his television set, he saw the actress displayed in full glory. Interestingly, there were no phone calls or complaints about this indiscretion.

Language

Constraints on language range from the obvious exorcising of profanity and racially derogatory remarks to the highly subjective area of slang. This generates many arguments between writers and standards executives over why _ass_ is acceptable but _tush_ is not, and why it is acceptable for someone to seek _protection_ before sex but the words _prophylactic_ and _condom_ are banned.

Sometimes writers and producers inject seemingly innocent statements with double entendres. Censors have learned to watch for these and to check on phrases spoken in a foreign language.

Early Evening Program Concerns

With primetime programming beginning at eight o'clock (seven in the central time zone), standards executives are particularly concerned about the number of children watching these early evening shows. Accordingly, they are increasingly stringent in their monitoring of these shows. They are much more lenient when dealing with adult shows such as _Miami Vice_ and _Hill Street Blues_, which air a bit later.

Sometimes, however, this zealousness is misplaced. A classic case was the NBC standards executive who wrote a serious memo declaring that the miniseries "Greatest Heroes of the Bible" could not be broadcast at eight o'clock because the story content was too violent for children. The executive recanted when the series producer threatened to release the memo to the newspapers.

PRESSURE GROUPS

The second major influence on network program content is the various individuals and public-interest groups who gain visibility by monitoring network programming. Although some of these groups are self-serving, many play an important role in helping correct misplaced sensibilities and ethnic stereotypes. Special-interest and pressure groups usually focus on four areas of television content: portrayal of minorities, amount of violence, suitability for children, and wholesomeness of programming.

Portrayal of Minorities

In the early history of movies and television, stereotypes and bigoted portrayals of minorities were prevalent. These included the shuffling black servant, epitomized by Stepin Fetchit, whose most frequent expression was "Yassir," who was not very bright and was easily scared, and who fled by screaming, "Feets, do yoah stuff!" Then there was the Frito Bandito, a negative stereotype of a Latino, and the inscrutable Charlie Chan, an Oriental stereotype.

The outrage against stereotyping began with the civil rights movement in the 1960s. It concentrated first on the portrayal of black Americans. Organizations were formed to monitor the media and correct the then−prevalent perception that blacks were slow witted and held only menial jobs. Up until that time, most black actors found themselves typecast as servants, dimwits, or heavies. The attention ultimately led to positive role models, including Bill Cosby in the television series *I Spy* and Diahann Carroll in *Julia*.

Noting the success of the black pressure groups, Latinos had early success in eliminating the popular but stereotypical commercial character known as the Frito Bandito. Italian-Americans fought to have the word *mafia* eliminated from television dialogue. Other groups, including gay rights activists, Orientals, and the Gray Panthers, also have brought pressure to bear on the networks to eliminate stereotyped portrayals.

Today a multitude of special-interest groups periodically demands attention from the network broadcast standards departments. Although such groups are justified in their desire to see more positive, well-rounded portrayals, the cumulative effect on programming can lead to yet another form of censorship. At one point, when black pressure groups were most active, writers and producers could not use a black man in a role as an antagonist. These constraints limited balanced casting opportunities for black actors, and as a result, the strictures were slowly lifted.

The most important role of broadcast standards departments in this area is ensuring that minorities are portrayed in a variety of roles. Just as white actors can be "good" or "bad" guys, dimwitted or sharp as a whip, crazy or sane, minority actors should be given the same opportunities to portray a broad range of characters. That is the goal of most special-interest groups.

Of course, some pressure groups are determined to keep all negative portrayals off network television. The consequence has been that many heavies on television are now motivated by some psychosis. No matter what their cultural background, they are not responsible for their actions. This type of portrayal is just as unrealistic as earlier stereotyped roles.

Amount of Violence

Two seemingly unanswerable questions plague the networks, producers, and public-interest groups: "What amount of violence is acceptable?" and "What constitutes violence?" Under the stringent conditions suggested by some of the most extreme groups, children's literature from the Grimm fairy tales to classics such as *Treasure Island* would be unacceptable. Further, there does not seem to be any differentiation between acts of violence. Hitting characters with a cream pie is as offensive as garroting them on screen. Broadcast standards departments must walk a thin line between allowing potentially harmful violence to remain in a show and removing relatively innocuous acts of violence in response to pressure from extreme groups. It is not an enviable task.

Suitability for Children

Recognizing that children are highly impressionable and consume great quantities of television, a number of groups monitor the content of children's programming, both on Saturday morning and during prime-time. With the aid of psychologists and sociologists, these groups are a strong force in determining the suitability of programming, as well as the quantity and type of advertisements, presented to children.

Much of these groups' effort centers on the prosocial values that can be intertwined in storytelling. They are primarily concerned about achieving positive portrayals of children as role models and avoiding the negative impact of frightening story elements.

Wholesomeness of Programming

While concerns about violence and the portrayal of minorities have prescribed goals, the issue of wholesomeness is more elusive. Nevertheless, it has become the platform for a number of organizations and several religious figures. Generally these organizations fear that "corrupt" television programs will bring about the destruction of American society. Although these groups certainly have a right to their opinions, wholesomeness is not, as yet, something network executives can monitor to the degree these groups desire.

12

Business Deals, License Fees, and Syndication

No matter how exciting a concept is, it cannot move to the next stage if terms cannot be satisfactorily negotiated. Business affairs departments at studios and networks are constantly engaged in constructing deals for every phase of programming, from development through network licensing.

When a producer has a commitment for a pilot or series, the business affairs office concludes negotiations with the agents for individual directors and actors in accordance with appropriate guild agreements (Writers Guild of America, Directors Guild of America, American Federation of TV and Radio Artists, American Federation of Musicians). Business deals include agreements concerning specific artistic services, credits, fees, royalties, and residuals.

A more complex and far-reaching process is undertaken by networks and studios when they engage in negotiations over the rights to a new series. Once a network is interested in a project, intensive negotiations take place concerning creative rights, network approvals, license fees, and residuals. The network license agreement that is finally resolved has an enormous impact on the producer's financial and creative ability to produce the series.

Among the more significant issues confronting the producer in negotiations are these present and future concerns: license fees, deficit financing, escalating production costs, star demands and network favors, and residuals and profits.

LICENSE FEES

License agreements set the formal legal basis for series ownership and control. These agreements define the ground rules for the right to air the series, the number of runs permitted (usually two), and the fees paid to the producer for production of each episode.

Negotiations on license fees can be fierce; they can make or break a project. Program license agreements can run two years or more. During that period, the network has exclusive rights to the project, including elements of creative control. The license fee negotiated generally falls far below the cost of actual production, and producers find themselves in the uncomfortable position of deficit financing.

Costs of production continually escalate, but the network license fee covers only a portion of the production costs for each episode. Currently, a one-hour filmed show costs approximately $1 million to produce. Stylish or action-filled shows and location-based programs such as *Miami Vice* cost considerably more. Yet the network license fee is much smaller. According to *Variety*, which lists estimated license fees per episode each season, ABC paid $725,000 for *MacGyver* and *Spenser for Hire*. Aaron Spelling negotiated a more generous $775,000 for *Hotel* and $950,000 for *The Colbys*, but the production costs still far outweighed the license fee arrangement.*

The same *Variety* survey revealed that NBC paid similar fees for its one-hour shows: $725,000 for *Remington Steele* and *Hunter*; $750,000 for *Blacke's Magic*; $775,000 for *Knight Rider*; and $800,000 for *Miami Vice* and *St. Elsewhere*.

CBS license fees followed the same pattern: $725,000 for *Murder, She Wrote* and $750,000 for *Cagney & Lacey*. With respect to prime-time soaps, Lorimar Productions negotiated higher per episode fees— $800,000 for *Knots Landing*; $850,000 for *Falcon Crest*; and $950,000 for *Dallas*.

Producers of half-hour shows face the same dilemma but to a lesser degree. Shows taped with three cameras on a stage and a live audience can be done cheaply with little deficit. According to *Variety's* primetime survey, ABC paid $325,000 for *Who's the Boss*; $350,000 for *Webster*; and $400,000 for *Diff'rent Strokes*.

NBC's range was similar for half-hour shows: $325,000 for *The Golden Girls*; $375,000 for *Night Court*; and $400,000 each for *Family Ties*, *The Facts of Life*, and *Cheers*. The upper scale of negotiated fees was $450,000 for the independently produced *The Cosby Show*. CBS license fees fell into the same financial category for half-hour series:

_____

*"1985–86 Network Primetime Season at a Glance," *Variety*, 25 September 1985; 50, 53, 55, 100,102.

$325,000 for *Foley Square*; $375,000 for *Mary* (MTM); and $400,000 for *Newhart*.

With series production costs spiraling, the network license fee can hardly meet the major costs of series production.

DEFICIT FINANCING

The problem of deficit financing is a serious one. As the costs of production escalate, so does the producer's extraordinary financial commitment. Networks have been reluctant to pick up substantial production costs for one-hour filmed shows, and smaller independent producers are being squeezed out. They simply cannot afford the deficits accumulated over the duration of the license agreement.

Major studios have barely been able to keep up with the deficit financing crunch, as they can face deficits of up to $400,000 per episode. If the network purchases 22 shows, the studio is committed to financing—at a loss—the additional $8.8 million dollars.

Since license fees have such an enormous financial impact, producers and networks battle for their negotiated rights. If they cannot agree on license fees, the show might never be seen. Some pilots have been ordered but never made it to screen because license fees could not be negotiated. The series either would have cost the network too much or driven a producer close to bankruptcy.

If the network wants to renegotiate the license agreement for a successful series, the process can result in vigorous arguments. Once a series is popular, the producer might not want to relinquish control and certainly does not want to operate in a deficit financing position. Sometimes, as the battle heats up, the network decides it would be wiser to drop a successful series than pay a higher license fee.

ESCALATING PRODUCTION COSTS

Producers are expected to work within established budgets for a series, but costs inevitably escalate for a variety of reasons. Among the factors are stars' demands, location shooting, union requirements, production problems, and technical costs.

A production budget is carefully detailed, accounting for every foreseeable need. It lists all the creative and technical requirements of the show. The budget in Figure 12–1 is typical, outlining above the line and below the line costs. *Above the line* refers to all creative elements, including writers, story, producer, director, and talent. *Below the line* designates all technical requirements.

UNIVERSAL CITY STUDIOS, INC.
PRODUCTION BUDGET

Scope:

Neg. Ft: Budget Date: _____

| Series (Production) Title | Episode Title | Production No. |

| Producer | Director |

Principals

SHOOTING SCHEDULE

| Start Date | Finish Date | Production Est. Days | Production Act. Days |

Days	REHEARSE	- STUDIO -			LOCAL LOCATION	DISTANT LOCATION	TRAVEL	IDLE		HOLIDAY	TOTAL
		STAGE	B/LOT	PROCESS				LAYOFF	SUNDAYS		
1st. Unit											
2nd. Unit											

COMMENTS

ACKNOWLEDGED

Approved for Production _____   Date _____

Figure 12–1.   Sample production budget form for Universal Studios.

When it comes to production, everything that can go wrong will go wrong. Weather might be bad on location, holding up production for days. Someone inevitably gets sick, and schedules must be reshuffled to accommodate everyone on the set. Directors might need to reshoot

Production Budget –					
ACCT. NO.	DESCRIPTION	PAGE NO.	BUDGET		
801	Story & Other Rights	2			
803	Writing	2			
805	Producer & Staff	2			
807	Director & Staff	3			
809	Talent	3			
810	Fringe Benefits	3			
TOTAL – ABOVE THE LINE					
811	Production Staff	4			
813	Camera	5			
814	Art Department	6			
815	Set Construction & Striking	6			
816	Special Effects	7			
817	Set Operations	8			
819	Electrical	9			
821	Set Dressing	10			
823	Action Props	11			
825	Livestock & Picture Vehicles	11			
827	Special Photography	12			
831	Wardrobe	13			
833	Makeup & Hairdressing	14			
835	Sound (Production)	15			
837	Locations (Local & Distant)	16			
838	Video Tape (Production)	17			
839	Transportation (Studio)	18			
841	Film (Production)	19			
845	Sundry & Tests	19			
847	Second Unit	20			
848	Insert Shooting	20			
TOTAL – SHOOTING PERIOD					
851	Editing & Projection	21			
852	Video Tape (Post Production)	22			
853	Music	23			
855	Sound (Post Production)	24			
857	Film & Stock Shots	25			
859	Titles, Optical, Inserts	26			
TOTAL – COMPLETION PERIOD					
861	Insurance	26			
863	Fringe Benefits	27			
866	Unit Publicist & Stillman	27			
867	General Expenses	28			
TOTAL – OTHER					
TOTAL – BELOW THE LINE					
TOTAL ABOVE & BELOW THE LINE (711)					
INDIRECT COST					
GRAND TOTAL					
PRODUCTION NO: EPISODE NO: DATE: PATTERN TOTAL:					

Figure 12–1.   (*continued*).

scenes when actors are no longer available. Editors might require close-up coverage that was not provided. Location clearances that were assured are not forthcoming. Artistic egos clash, and someone walks off the set. Long-planned production schedules might suddenly conflict.

FIRST REPORT

MCA TELEVISION/ESTIMATED PRODUCTION COST REPORT

Production Number:	Series:	Title:			Episode Number:	Date
62210					3	TUE August 12, 1986

Director:	Pattern:	Budget this show:	Current (under) OVER Budget
	1,231,018	1,231,006	2,240

FIRST REPORT - COMPLETION OF PHOTOGRAPHY

		Est Final	Hours Budget	Hours Worked	Pages Sched	Pages Shot
1ST RPT		1,233,246	80.0	74.3	48 6/8	48 6/8
5WK						
12WK						
EST FIN						

Remarks:
RATE CARD BUDGET. BUDGET INCLUDES WRITERS' SALARIES AT $6,419 OVER PATTERN.

SHOOTING PERIOD 08/01/86 - 08/11/86.
08/12/86 - 1ST REPORT - Adj. $2,240.
OVERAGES DUE TO:
- Locations - Set watch and harbor warden - 2,438.

STATUS:
COMPLETED PRINCIPAL PHOTOGRAPHY ON SCHEDULE

$2,240 - Over budget
$2,228 - Over pattern

Hours budgeted - 80.0
Hours worked - 74.3

THESE ESTIMATES REFLECT PRODUCTION SHOOTING COSTS ONLY AND ARE PREDICATED UPON ALL POST PRODUCTION, GROUP AND AMORTIZED COSTS ADHERING TO BUDGET

Figure 12-2. Sample daily production cost report for an hour-long action TV series.

Facilities required might not be available. Rates for insurance coverage soar. Stars argue about the size of their dressing rooms or credits, and they might stalk off the set.

Production companies keep a daily log of estimated production costs and overage (budget overruns). Figure 12−2 shows a sample production cost report for a one−hour action series. The *pattern budget* refers to the typical costs per episode ($1,231,018). This report shows the program is already over budget ($2,240). According to the report, the problems were related to unexpected location requirement needs (set watch and harbor warden).

If it is possible to disrupt production *and* increase the costs in the process, it will happen. One of the most expensive production commitments for ABC is *Moonlighting*, an ABC in-house series. Since the network has a vested interest in it, they lavish more production money on it and permit an exceptionally long and expensive twelve-day shooting schedule. Networks traditionally rely on outside producers to hold the line on production problems and series budgets, so they have no real experience in these areas. As a result, the production problems escalate and the producing group is unable to make airdate deadlines. In 1986 the network was forced to air repeat episodes during the crucial February sweeps, shows were delivered short of acceptable running time, and the budget shot up astronomically.

STAR DEMANDS AND NETWORK FAVORS

Once a series is popular, stars inevitably want a larger piece of the action. They feel (perhaps rightly) that they are largely responsible for the success of the series. As a result, agents demand higher salaries and other perks for their clients. Producers and networks think the salaries are already high enough. New demands can seriously undermine a tenuous series budget.

If the demands are taken seriously, the network might offer a production commitment to the star for one or two new projects. For example, Gary Coleman and Johnny Carson were guaranteed on-air production commitments in lieu of higher salaries. These commitments allow the star to form a production company with a guaranteed network commitment for the new projects. The stars themselves are not required to appear in the new projects. Additionally they serve as tax incentives since the income is deferred.

The networks offer the same type of deal to successful production company executives. If a producer has a strong primetime track record, the network might want the right of first refusal for all new shows and might guarantee the producer a production commitment. Aaron Spelling has a five-year deal with ABC guaranteeing him a new series every year. CBS wanted exclusive rights to Lorimar productions (which include *Dallas* and *Knots Landing*), so they negotiated a right of first refusal on new shows plus a guarantee of pilot production for new projects.

Even network executives can benefit from this. It is common practice for key executives to negotiate terms for their eventual separation from the network. They might be guaranteed a certain number of scripts or even a pilot when they leave the network. That makes them powerful instant production companies, holding the most golden of apples: a network commitment for new programming.

RESIDUALS AND PROFITS

Only after a show has run on the network for the license period (two runs) can producers hope to recoup costs. The long and costly production gambit can be worth it if the series builds an established audience and a large number of episodes are produced. Established series can be sold into syndication—the prime marketplace for profit. Other marketplaces include pay television and foreign television distribution.

Syndication

Syndication is where producers can hopefully recoup the cost of production and earn significant profits. Syndicated programs can be sold to independent television stations around the country, as well as to network affiliates.

According to the Association of Independent Television Stations (INTV), syndicated program sales exceeded $1.2 billion in 1985 alone. They estimated 270 independent stations around the country required 36,000 hours of programming by 1987 and that that figure would climb to 40,000 hours by 1990.* There is a massive need for programming to satiate the needs of independent station programmers.

With the number of independent stations and affiliates growing, there has been an increase in the demand for programs. Traditionally, programming sales required many series episodes for *stripping* (airing daily on independent stations). More recently, producers have found syndicators more amenable to short-run series as well.

Producers (studios and production companies) also offer innova-

---

*"Syndication Follies and the San Andreas Fault," *Merrill Lynch Entertainment Industry Reports*, 7 February 1985, 1–2.

tive packages to syndicators, combining different shows with similar themes. A package called "Summer Gold," offered by Golden West, was comprised of three short-lived series (*It's a Living, I'm a Big Girl Now,* and *It Takes Two*). It was a successful syndication package of episodic comedy for the summer schedule.

Movie packages also are prime sources of syndication efforts. MCA (owner of Universal Studios) compiled "Mystery Movies" (124 episodes from their film library). MGM/UA put together "MGM/UA Premiere Network," a package of 24 films. Embassy packaged 8 films under the title "Embassy Night at the Movies." These movie packages generated ad revenues of $1 million to $2 million per film.*

Due to supply and demand, prices for syndicating very successful network shows can be extremely high, earning enormous profits for the producers. As reported in a Standard & Poor's survey, *Magnum, P.I.*, a one-hour action series, entered syndication in 1986 with a price tag of $1.6 million per episode. *Cheers*, a half-hour comedy series, entered syndication in 1987 at a cost of more than $1 million per episode.**

In the syndication marketplace, half-hour comedies have become extremely popular. This is the result of two factors. First, prior to the debut of *The Cosby Show*, situation comedy was a failing form on network television. None ranked in the top ten of network series. Consequently, few comedies lasted on the air long enough to form a syndication package (usually three years).

This scarcity was compounded by a second factor. At the 1986 conference of the National Association of Television Program Executives (NATPE), one trade publication ran a report on the endurance of situation comedies, concluding that they clearly dominate the syndicated market.*** Half-hour situation comedies generate higher syndicated ratings than one-hour shows and provide the station with more flexibility in scheduling.

This report, and several others like it, had an enormous impact on the 1986 conference and radically affected the syndication marketplace. Station managers turned away from drama programs and sought to purchase situation comedies almost exclusively.

As a result, in an almost perfect example of the free enterprise supply and demand system, prices for comedies reached new heights. In 1985 *Silver Spoons* earned Embassy more than $55 million in gross sales at stations in 10 major markets. *Webster* earned Paramount a record-breaking $135 million in 75 markets, and the producers received $1.3

Standard & Poor's Industry Surveys, 27 June 1985, 4.

**Ibid, 2.

***Electronic Media*, 11 November 1985, 1, 27.

million per half-hour episode. Yet both these series were weak performers in their first-run network ratings competition. In the 1985 primetime season, *Silver Spoons* averaged a 10.4 rating and *Webster* a 17 rating, both far below competitive levels. According to a Los Angeles station manager interviewed for a trade paper report, off-network situation comedies have become so valuable to stations that "even the bad ones become good."*

A peak was reached in 1987 when *The Cosby Show* was introduced to syndication on a closed bid basis. When negotiations are completed for all markets around the country, the revenue received for the show is expected to exceed any program in history.

The marketplace for drama programs, however, is not as auspicious. *Magnum's* sale in 1985 seems to have been the pinnacle for the form. New drama series vying for syndication sales have met strong resistance. This is especially true for programs such as *Cagney and Lacy* and *Miami Vice*. While extremely successful in their respective network runs, independent stations find they can only be played in the late evening hours. Since many of the stations run movies from 8 to 10 P.M. (Eastern and Pacific time) and air their evening newscast at 10 P.M., adult programs like these must be placed in relatively low viewing periods of 11 P.M. and after.

The syndication of highly popular series can be very costly for independent stations. For this reason, deals for series and movie packages often involve a process called *bartering*. Bartering helps stations acquire competitive programming with virtually no cash-flow problems. Under a barter arrangement, the program is offered to stations in exchange for a prescribed number of commercial minutes that can be sold to national advertisers.

A typical barter arrangement for a one-hour show includes six minutes of advertising sold by the distributor and six minutes sold by the independent station. In this case, advertising revenues can be exceptionally high. According to Standard & Poor's, advertising volume under barter arrangements will reach $660 million in 1987 and climb to more than $1 billion in 1990. Barter syndication is big business.**

Falcon Crest was one of the first recent vintage off-network one-hour strips offered on a straight barter basis. In that arrangement, Lorimar received five minutes of advertising per episode, and the local station received seven minutes of advertising. According to Standard and Poor's, Lorimar presumably chose the barter route because of a lack of

---

*Electronic Media, 11 November 1985, 27.
**Standard & Poor's Industry Surveys, 27 June 1985, 1.

interest from major market affiliates, despite a respectable percentage of clearance from local stations for *Dallas*.*

Serials tend to perform poorly in rerun situations because the core audience already is familiar with the plot. For this reason, daytime soap operas remain in continuous production; they never repeat episodes. Similarly, networks usually remove serial dramas from their schedules in the summer to avoid having to run repeats.

In addition to reruns and packaged films, syndicators have new programming produced exclusively for the syndicated market. One early experiment involved the revival of popular series that failed to sustain network commitments. Series such as *Fame* and *Too Close for Comfort* were resurrected and successfully produced for the syndicated market.

In 1986 a host of new situation comedies premiered, conceived and produced directly for first–run syndication. Some of them, such as *Small Wonder* and *Throb*, became quite successful ratings achievers. This has stimulated the introduction of even more first-run sitcoms.

The NATPE conventions are a program manager's delight, an enormous bazaar filled with potential new programs as well as packages of feature movies and old network series. In the past few years the most popular new programs are heavily oriented toward game formats, talk shows, and situation comedies. Some of the most successful are *Wheel of Fortune, Solid Gold, Jeopardy, Donahue, Oprah Winfrey, Entertainment Tonight, The People's Court,* and *Divorce Court.*

Sometimes syndication groups even try miniseries, although such ventures are particularly expensive. Operation Primetime, a consortium of mostly independent stations, produce two miniseries annually. In 1987 they developed "The Life of Henry Ford" and "Hoover vs. Kennedy." In that same year Taft independent stations dropped out of the consortium. Despite internal problems and escalating production budgets, Al Masini, founder of Operation Primetime and President of Telerep, predicted a strong future for the enterprise.**

Major studios and production companies have become increasingly more active in non-network production. As one reflection of that interest, 20th Century Fox Corporation announced the formation of the Fox Broadcasting Company to produce and distribute original programming across the country to their own assemblage of stations and to a group of affiliated stations. While technically not a new network because they only intend to program two nights a week, the programming format and intent is identical to network practices. In October, 1986 they premiered

---

*Television/Radio Age, 25 November 1985, 49.

**"OPT Weblet Orders Two Minis For '87; Taft Indies Resign," Variety, 14 January 1987, 141.

their first show, the late night *Joan Rivers Show*, which competes in many markets with NBC's *Johnny Carson Show*.

Other Sources of Distribution

Producers of new programs also can bring those shows to the pay cable marketplace. Only a few cable companies can financially compete for television and film programming. Among them are HBO and Showtime. These two competitive giants have even entered into joint ventures with major studios to protect their pay window (exclusivity) for new motion pictures produced by those studios, along with older films on studio shelves.

Additionally, the advertiser-supported basic cable services, such as WTBS, the USA Network, and the Arts and Entertainment Network, have become the purchaser of old network series and even first-run programming. In 1987 WTBS was running expressly produced episodes of *The New Leave It to Beaver*, and USA Network premiered original episodes of *Alfred Hitchcock Presents*.

In addition to the syndicated and pay cable markets, network programming is sold to the foreign market. Some distributors are set up exclusively to sell to Western Europe, the Far East, and Central America. Many foreign broadcasters find American television fare inexpensive and surprisingly successful. It is not unusual for broadcasters in places such as Hong Kong to air vintage American series in their current primetime schedules.

The History and Impact of Technology on Programming Trends

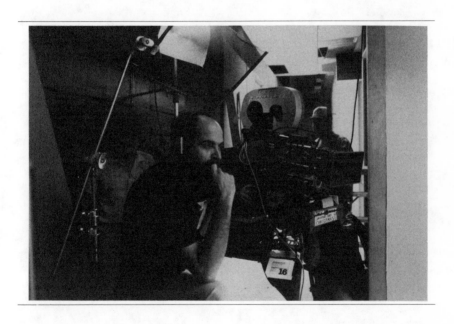

The Effects of Technology on Television Programming

After more than sixty years, it is difficult to remember that the networks initially were formed as a solution to a technological problem of the 1920s. In those days, radio stations were independent entities, relying solely on their own resources for program material. The only available recording device was the phonograph record. But while playing records on radio was common, the equipment to make records was costly and difficult to operate. As a consequence, few stations had any recording capability.

The need for programming, as well as the exciting prospect of hearing live broadcasts from another city, created the desire to share programs with other radio stations. Since the telephone company was an early proponent of radio, it was not long before stations in New York (WEAF) and Boston (WNAC) were connected by a telephone line (January 4, 1923). This was the beginning of networking.

Just a few years later, on November 1, 1926, the National Broadcasting Company (NBC) was formed, and in a few years, the entire country, from coast to coast, could simultaneously listen to the same radio broadcast. More importantly, for people within the fledgling industry there now existed a distribution system for originally produced entertainment programs.

The process was so successful that it generated four national networks—the NBC red and blue networks (the latter ultimately became

ABC); CBS, founded in 1927; and the Mutual Network, founded in 1936. By the late 1940s, the big three had expanded into television, but it was not until the 1950s that advances in microwave technology permitted the instantaneous transmission of visual images across the country. Television viewers were treated to shows such as *Wide, Wide World*. Every Sunday they could watch events across the country live from the comfort of their living rooms. They also saw live, prestigious dramas such as *Playhouse 90*.*

Ultimately, microwave towers were supplemented by coaxial cables and satellites, and the pictures became sharper and colorful. But despite the enormous technological advances and the ability by all to record, store, and play back video programming at any time, few people within the television industry seemed to recognize that the concept of interconnecting stations for simultaneous program distribution was no longer necessary or even desirable. Indications are that television in the 1990s will be strongly affected by the turning away from mass media networks and the trend toward fragmentation and specialization.

FACTORS CONTRIBUTING TO CHANGE

Three major factors are the driving force behind the current evolution of television. They are technology, audience fragmentation, and the changed regulatory environment.

Technology

The difficulty of cutting records during the formative days of networking has been eliminated by the enormous advances in electronics of the past half century. Today anyone can make an audio recording, and the equipment is excellent, portable, and inexpensive. In the past ten years, this capability has extended into video, where a machine weighing less than four pounds can record with available light exceptional pictures in color and include stereo sound. Remarkably, the cost of such a camcorder is less than the purchase price of a black-and-white television set in 1950.

_____

*For more on the history of broadcasting, see Erik Barnouw, *Tube of Plenty: The Evolution of American Television* (New York: Oxford University Press, 1982); Les Brown, *Encyclopedia of Television* (New York: Zoetrope, 1982); Sydney W. Head and Christopher H. Sterling, *Broadcasting in America: A Survey of Electronic Media*, 5th ed. (Boston: Houghton-Mifflin, 1986); Lawrence Lichty and Malachi Topping, *American Broadcasting: A Source Book on the History of Radio and Television* (New York: Hastings House, 1975). For additional resources see Annotated Bibliography.

Still, most people do not make their own programming. They turn to some available source to meet their entertainment needs. In the past, they have turned primarily to the three national networks, but the networks now face increasingly more powerful opponents.

Cable Television

Cable television began with the simple sharing of an antenna by people in rural areas who could not receive a good signal from a distant television station. It usually was installed by some telephone repairman or a television appliance merchant.

The idea quickly spread, with communities running wires down the street to share the cost and reap the rewards of better reception. This is the origin of the term *community antenna television*, or CATV. Unrecognized was the fact that the coaxial cable used to tie together these households was capable of transmitting many more channels than the major networks plus a public broadcasting station (PBS) and perhaps a nearby independent station.

As the cable companies installed more sophisticated equipment, they slowly began to find uses for the extra capacity. Typically one channel focused a camera on a small weather station, showing temperature, pressure, and wind readings. Another scanned past three-by-five cards containing announcements of local events or sales. Local community events, such as basketball games and city council meetings, were broadcast on an unused channel.

In some cases, because of terrain and certain microwave networks, residents discovered that the head-end antennas could bring in the signals of very distant stations. This importation of distant stations evolved into superstations such as WTBS and WOR. Today the typical thirty-channel or more cable systems are found in many communities across the country, competing vigorously with broadcast stations for the attention (and subscriber fees) of countless households.

Pay Television

Experiments with over-the-air subscription or pay television date back to the 1950s. They failed at that time because of technical problems, strong resistance from broadcast stations and networks, and a lack of adequate programming. The emergence of cable television in the 1970s provided a new impetus for pay programming. Companies in Los Angeles and a few other markets negotiated with movie studios to play feature films unedited and uninterrupted at an additional charge to cable subscribers, which the cable company then shared with the movie distributor. The popularity of such offerings vastly increased the number of cable subscribers in areas where there was no difficulty receiving over-the-air broadcasts.

Recognizing that pay television was very popular with the public, the cable companies expanded into major cities. Cable systems began offering a choice of two or three pay services, the so-called multitier pay approach. Where no widespread cable service was available, UHF stations used scrambling and decoder equipment to begin over-the-air pay operations.

In such a rapidly growing environment, many regional pay companies were absorbed into large national services such as Home Box Office (HBO), Showtime, Cinemax, and The Movie Channel. In the past few years, with other technology entering the marketplace, the growth of pay cable has slowed.

Video Players

After a flurry of announcements in the 1970s following Sony's development of the U-matic three-quarter-inch video recorder/player, it was widely assumed that home video would become the billion-dollar industry of 1975. The high cost of the machine (well over $1,000), combined with the high cost of tape (over $30) and short play time (one hour), limited the consumer market to wealthy videophiles. The three-quarter-inch machine, however, ultimately gained wide acceptance in industrial applications and became the professional standard for non-studio video equipment.

Not until the simultaneous development of the half-inch videotape machine and the laser disc player in the early 1980s did video begin to make inroads into the home. While the resolution and sound quality of the laser disc systems was superior, and studios and production entities liked the copyright protection, the general public turned to tape recorders, which offered the ability to record programs off the air.

The popularization of the video recorder/players encouraged the videotape rental business, where for a price substantially less than the cost of a single movie ticket, people could rent a recent motion picture for viewing in the comfort and privacy of their homes. Video stores have spread like fleas across the landscape, with many companies installing their own video rental libraries, where employees can pick up an evening's entertainment on the way home and return it the next morning.

Station Proliferation

As television became popular, the demand for new stations quickly outstripped the allocated broadcast spectrum of channels 2 through 13. The introduction of the UHF spectrum theoretically provided for an expansion of the number of stations. But the need for a separate antenna and tuners, along with the poorer propagation of the UHF signal, made these stations pale in comparison to the big, already successful VHF channels.

The emergence of cable, where all signals, UHF and VHF, were available to the viewer through an easy-to-use converter box, finally brought parity and concurrent economic survival to the UHF outlets. Cable access, combined with loosened FCC restrictions on the number of stations allowed within a geographic area, has dramatically increased the number of broadcast stations in the United States.

Satellites

In the 1960s the launch of the first communications satellite, *Telestar*, amazed television viewers with the first live pictures from Europe. In the ensuing two decades, communications satellites have evolved from crude, complex, expensive devices to effective, very inexpensive methods of transmitting high-quality television programs around the country and around the world. Today almost all television programming at one stage or another passes through a satellite, either while it is being sent to a network, being transmitted by a network, or being beamed to a particular location.

Satellite technology also allowed the formation of new kinds of networks: those consisting of a single station and those that have no stations at all. Several independent stations in large markets, starting with WTBS in Atlanta, became superstations, beaming their signals directly to satellites for access to cable systems across the country and selling advertising based on their national coverage. After beginning with a program structure composed of old movies and music videos, they have now begun producing original programming just like the three big networks.

Basic cable networks require no broadcast station at all, instead relying on satellites to feed their signal to cable system head-ends and homes with satellite dishes. Advertising supported, like the superstations, they usually specialize in particular program forms—CNN for news, MTV for music videos, ESPN for sports, ARTS & Entertainment (A & E) for cultural programs. There are also religious networks, weather networks, health networks, and cable networks programming old movies and old network series.

The ability to receive satellite transmissions in the home also has progressed. While at first costing many thousands of dollars and requiring the installation of large dish antennas, in 1986 an unobtrusive dish antenna with an equipment cost of about five hundred dollars could provide any home with the capability to receive hundreds of channels of programming. But as low-cost satellite dishes have begun to proliferate, pay television services and networks have begun to scramble their signals to prevent unauthorized access to their material.

Audience Fragmentation

As Alvin Toffler effectively pointed out in his best-selling book, *Future Shock*, technology's ability to provide an ever-increasing array of choices has produced fragmentation in American society.* In the print media, this fragmentation has led from general-interest mass media forms to a multitude of specialized choices. The magazine business has gone from a few big national periodicals such as *Life*, *Look*, and *The Saturday Evening Post* to hundreds of special-interest magazines ranging from *Byte* and *Motor Trend* to *Playboy*, *Forbes*, *Tiger Beat*, and *Omni*, to mention just a few.

While similar expansion and segmentation were occurring throughout American culture, television viewing continued to be governed by the limited number of broadcast stations permitted by technology and regulations. Network television became the last truly mass medium, where viewers often chose Paul Klein's famous "least objectionable program" because nothing else was available.

The advent of cable, video players, and satellites has removed viewing restrictions. As a consequence, if none of the programs on the big three networks is appealing, the viewer is likely to explore other choices, whether it be CNN, MTV, an independent station, or a videocassette. The result has been a dramatic decline in network viewing share, as shown in Figure 13−1.

The trend is clear: More choices and more specialized choices are now available. Already a cable viewer can choose a channel that shows only movies, features just music, programs exclusively to children, broadcasts the latest news at any hour, focuses solely on sporting events, or shows the national government in action. Videocassettes broaden the choices even further, with tapes ranging from health and fitness to pornography. The future holds even more options. With all these choices, audiences can view what they want to watch when they want to watch it. In this way, television is beginning to resemble the highly specialized magazine field.

---

*Alvin Toffler, *Future Shock* (New York: Random House, 1970).

Changed Regulatory Environment

In the strong regulatory environment following the Communications Act
of 1934, both the number of broadcast stations and the ownership of
them was scrutinized by the FCC and the Justice Department. No individual or corporation was allowed to own more than five VHF stations

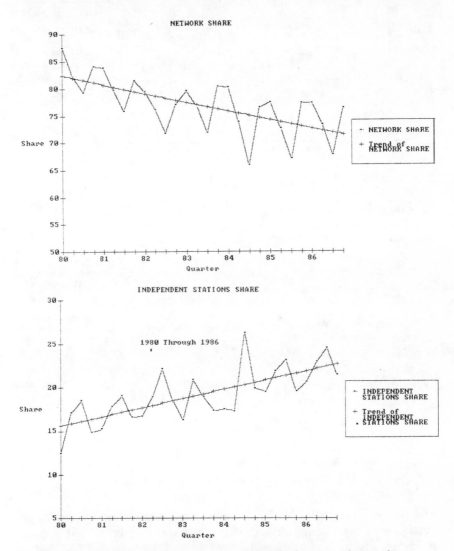

Figure 13—1.   The networks show a marked decline in audience share
compared to independent stations, pay cable, and basic cable.

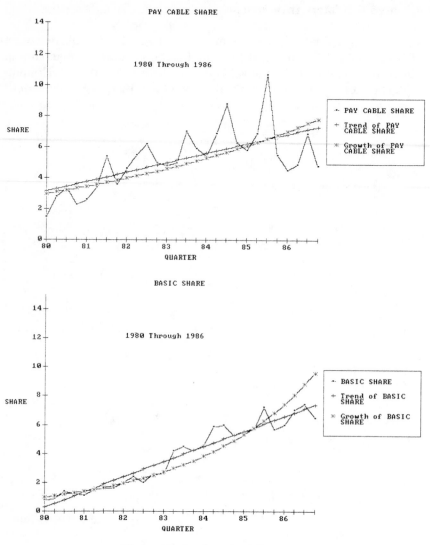

Figure 13−1.   (continued).

and two UHF stations. Networks were prohibited from owning cable systems, as were companies with newspapers or broadcast station holdings.

As a result, television station ownership remained an enormously profitable but still relatively small business. Most stations were owned by individuals or companies owning a few other stations. Similarly, while growing through merger, cable companies were kept separate from large equipment manufacturers or program suppliers.

The deregulatory environment following the election of Ronald Reagan in 1980 has dramatically changed this picture. A single entity can now own twelve stations, and the restrictions on cross-ownership have disappeared. Large corporations have begun making inroads on television station and cable ownership. By 1986 the Murdoch publishing empire had purchased a studio (20th Century Fox) and the former Metromedia television stations. The Tribune newspaper organization had purchased a host of stations forming the Tribune Broadcasting Company, and MCA, owner of Universal Studios, had bought superstation WOR.

THE NEAR FUTURE: IMMINENT TRENDS IN
PRIMETIME TELEVISION

Technological, sociological, and regulatory changes are changing the face of primetime television. Figure 13−2 demonstrates the fragmentation of television viewing as alternative forces have entered the marketplace. Threatening to accelerate the process are the following current developments.

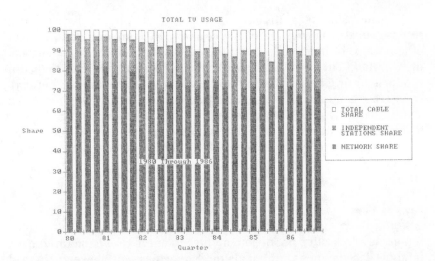

Figure 13−2. Over the years there has been a steady decline in viewers of network television.

New Networks

Recognizing that with low-cost satellite use, it is possible to provide programming to an array of independent stations across the nation, new networks are being planned. These will not be as large or comprehensive as the big three; instead, they will be alignments of stations to distribute one or more programs simultaneously across the country.

The most ambitious enterprise is The Fox Network. Having established its presence in television with the purchase of 20th Century Fox studios and the former Metromedia station group, Rupert Murdoch is actively pursuing the formation of a true fourth national network. Under the direction of Barry Diller, plans call for the initiation of two nights of programming in 1987, with expansion to other nights to follow.

First-Run Syndication

As prices have risen in the syndication marketplace, station owners have begun looking for alternative program sources. It is one thing to pay heavily for reruns of hit network series such as *Magnum, P.I.* and *The Cosby Show*, which have proven popularity and can be scheduled during any daypart. It is quite something else to pay large syndication fees for reruns of hour-long network series that were only marginally successful in their network runs and can be programmed only in the late evening.

The new station groups have discovered that by themselves they can reach a substantial portion of the country. By combining efforts with other groups of independent stations, they can easily achieve national distribution. This fact, combined with the knowledge that they can produce an original show for the same cost as they can buy network reruns, has generated a new, burgeoning market for originally produced syndicated programs. The impetus for first-run programming also has come from the ratings success of game shows, such as *Wheel of Fortune*, and inexpensive children-oriented situation comedies, such as *Small Wonder*.

Pay Per View

If there is a figurative pot of gold at the end of the television producer's rainbow, it is pay-per-view television, where the home viewer is charged incrementally for each show watched. Since people seem very willing to rent cassettes at a cost of two to five dollars, the economics are very simple. Suppose even 10 percent of the approximately 90 million television homes decide to watch a pay-per-view show. Overnight, the producers have grossed between 18 million and 45 million dollars. With satellites, only one print or tape of the show is needed, and distribution is instantaneous and inexpensive.

The concept of pay-per-view television began in the 1960s with sporting events sent by closed-circuit television to movie theaters, where patrons would pay to watch the events on the theater screen. As over-the-air pay television proliferated, organizations such as ON TV in Los Angeles scheduled a number of sporting events and the television premieres of big box office movies as pay-per-view events. They even went so far as to produce a movie, a filmed version of the *Pirates of Penzance*, especially for pay-per-view exhibition.

The results have been mixed. The public at first responded to the novelty of the idea but then chilled at having to pay individually for their television programs. It became evident that pay-per-view is highly dependent on the product itself. Viewers must find the event important and special enough to warrant the charge. Despite these potential problems, plans for regularly scheduled events are proceeding.

THE DISTANT FUTURE: PROJECTED TRENDS
FOR TELEVISION

Examining technological developments that could become commonplace in the next decade is challenging and risky. Only time will prove the accuracy of the forecasts. Among the developments seemingly headed our way are the following.

High-Definition Television

Undergoing extensive technological development for the past five years or so, high-definition television is already being used in industrial applications and is destined to become a consumer product. Various forms of high-definition television have been demonstrated at consumer and electronics showplaces, and the technical standards for this improved development are being ironed out.

High-definition television offers a picture substantially improved over what has been available. The U.S. standard, developed according to the technological expertise of the 1940s, provides 525 lines of resolution at the point of origin. By the time the signal reaches the average home, this resolution has dropped to fewer than 400 lines. As a consequence, resolution is relatively poor, a fact that is apparent on big-screen or projection television sets.

The high-definition television system standard provides twice that resolution, 1050 lines of picture information, and an aspect ratio that changes the standard television picture into the equivalent of a wide-screen movie format. The results are startling. The picture appears astoundingly sharp, bright, and almost three-dimensional. The arrival of high resolution will make large-screen television viewing commonplace.

Digital Television

The merging of computer technology with television is another example of our increasing dependence on computers in every aspect of contemporary American life. Digital television began with the space program, in which such devices sent the remarkable pictures of other planets and technicians developed the ability to use computers to enhance poor or unclear images.

Digital television replaces the conventional analog signal with a binary stream containing all the information needed for the picture and sound. Just as the digital sound of compact discs has eclipsed the analog long-playing record, the ability to transmit digital television signals will lead to the ultimate abandonment of the current system.

Digital technology offers a method of transmitting the broadcast signal, whether over the air, through satellites, or over coaxial cable, with virtually no loss of information. The computer enhancement ability of digitalization also will offer better color, less noise and distortion, and the elimination of ghost images. When combined with high-definition television, the two technologies can bring home a large-screen image every bit as good, if not better, than what is currently available in movie theaters.

Computer Television

The utilization of computers and new transmission technologies also will bring about the ultimate television system: instantaneous access to technically perfect multitudinous programming choices with total availability at any time of the day or night. The system would operate as follows. Every week the household would receive a guide, at first glance appearing similar to today's *TV Guide.* This guide would contain a library section, containing the permanent collection, and a temporary section, containing the current week's choices. The library section might consist of classic entertainment programs, instructional and educational programs, travelogues, exercise regimens, and do-it-yourself home repair demonstrations. The temporary section would contain announcements and advertisements for new movies, specials, and series episodes.

Each listing would have an associated address code. Some programs would be free and advertiser supported, just as they are in conventional television today. Other programs would contain noninterruptive advertising but would charge a nominal fee for access. Still other shows would be available only for pay.

Each home could choose the programs they want to watch at the time they want to watch them. The viewer would simply punch the address code into a special pad near the television. After a delay of perhaps a minute or two, the program would appear on the set.

How would the system work? The request code would be sent upstream to a computer, along with the specific code identifying the household. All the programs would be stored in digital form in the computer library. For each request received, the computer would access the program in its data bank library and send the signal by high-speed digital transmission down the line to the requesting household, where a digital videotape recorder built into the television set would record it. If a fee was associated with viewing, the computer would add it to the household's monthly bill, just as the telephone company does. The smart television set would then play back the videotaped signal in real time.

THE IMPACT OF TECHNOLOGY ON PROGRAMMING CONTENT

While it is challenging to speculate on future advances in the medium, any computer user will affirm that hardware without software is useless. The improvements discussed in this chapter have dealt with the technical ability (hardware) to provide new and more sophisticated distribution systems. They are useless, however, unless they are supported by programming (software).

In projecting the possible future of programming, the principal questions are supply and cost. As cable companies quickly learned, it is useless to have one hundred channels if there is no programming available for them (or the only programs accessible are failed versions of old network shows). Additionally, since programming can be very expensive, how will these new technologies afford the cost of programming on top of their major capital hardware expenses?

Increased Demand for Low-Cost Programming

None of the new station alignments or formative networks can afford the million-plus dollars per hour costs associated with primetime network programming. Stations such as Ted Turner's WTBS and cable networks such as USA have turned to low-cost producing entities to provide simple, economical programming. While Hollywood seems preoccupied with the technical quality of its product—color, lighting, camera moves, stereo sound, lush sets, extensive stunts, special effects—much of the television audience appears oblivious to these elements if provided with an attractive concept, likable characters, and appealing stories.

More Pay and Pay-Per-View Programming

The inevitable result of increased competition will be smaller, more fragmented audiences. As the television audience continues to desert the mass-appeal network offerings, it is unlikely that the prices paid by advertisers for network shows will rise much. Advertisers undoubtedly will disperse their funds to reach the maximum number of potential consumers.

Eventually, therefore, viewers probably will be called upon to support the shows they want to see. Pay programming is a viable companion to fragmented audiences. For example, perhaps there are a million or so railroad enthusiasts in the country—certainly not enough to provide a suitable base for traditional advertising support. It seems reasonable, however, that these railroad fans would be willing to pay several dollars occasionally to see programs devoted to the subject. That would make the project feasible and financially rewarding for a television production company.

Greater Differentiation of Network License Fees

A narrow range of about 10 percent ($100,000 for a one-hour show) has separated the most expensive new hour of network programming from the least expensive. Traditionally, producers of expensive shows have accepted a greater deficit in hopes of obtaining the return on investment from the syndication market.

With new networks and station groups competing against one another with original programming, the financial prospects for reruns of network shows in the syndication marketplace appear risky. Certainly there will always be an attractive market for proven successful winners such as *The Cosby Show, Miami Vice,* and *Magnum, P.I.* But the viability of less successful but still expensive programming is questionable.

It would seem, therefore, that the program distributor, whether network or station group, will have to assess program cost in conjunction with need. If they believe a high-action, location-based program is necessary, then they will have to be prepared to pay substantially more for it than for a relatively low-cost show, such as a courtroom drama.

Desirability of Programs with a Long Shelf Life

It is already apparent that some shows have a long life after their network exposure, whereas others disappear quickly from sight and mind. This factor will become more important in production decisions in the future.

The show with the longest shelf life is undoubtedly *I Love Lucy*, which has been on the air continuously for the thirty some-odd years since it halted production. Other shows with a proven shelf life are *The Twilight Zone, M*A*S*H, The Brady Bunch*, and *Star Trek*. Interestingly, shelf life does not seem to correlate with network success. *I Love Lucy* and *M*A*S*H* were enormously successful, but *The Twilight Zone* and *Star Trek* were not. Alternatively, some very highly rated network shows have done poorly in reruns, including *The Fugitive* and *Dallas*.

The criteria for shelf life appear to be the following:

1. The stories remain contemporary so that new, younger audiences can find and enjoy them.
2. The programs are set in a time period that does not make them seem dated.
3. The programs appeal to an audience of hard-core fans who do not tire of watching their favorite shows over and over again.
4. The shows appeal to young people. Walt Disney first demonstrated the principle of shelf life through the periodic re-releases of his animated classics.

New technologies and the increased demand for special programming together provide the promise that in the next decade, television will become an even more vibrant, exciting, and challenging medium.

Appendix: Trade Magazines, Journals, and Reports

Advertising Age
220 E. 42nd St.
New York, NY 10017

Adweek
ASM Communications, Inc.
820 Second Ave.
New York, NY 10017

Backstage
1411 Broadway
New York, NY 10036

Broadcasting
1735 DeSales St., N.W.
Washington, DC 20036

Cablevision
2500 Curtis St.
Denver, CO 80205

Channels
Box 2001
Mahopac, NY 10541

COMM/ENT: Journal of Communications and Entertainment Law
Hastings College of Law
San Francisco, CA 94111

Daily Variety
1400 N. Cahuenga Blvd.
Hollywood, CA 90028

Electronic Media
Crain Communications, Inc.
740 Rush St.
Chicago, IL 60611

Emmy
Academy of Television Arts and
   Sciences
4605 Lankershim Blvd.
North Hollywood, CA 91602

The Hollywood Reporter
6715 Sunset Blvd.
Hollywood, CA 90028

Journal of Broadcasting
Broadcast Education Association
1771 N St., N.W.
Washington, DC 20036

Journal of Communication
Annenberg School of Communication
Box 13358
3620 Walnut St., #C5
Philadelphia, PA 19104

*The Journal of Popular Film and
   Television*
Heldref Publications
4000 Albermarle St., N.W.
Washington, DC 20016

Media Report to Women
3306 Ross Place, N.W.
Washington, DC 20008

Merrill Lynch Capital Market Reports
Entertainment Industry Reports
Securities Research Division
Merrill Lynch, Pierce, Fenner & Smith,
   Inc.
Liberty Plaza
New York, NY 10011

Multichannel News
633 Third Ave.
New York, NY 10022

*Report on Prime Time Network
   Television*
Batten, Barton, Durstine & Osborne,
   Inc.
383 Madison Ave.
New York, NY 10017

Ross Reports
Television Index, Inc.
150 Fifth Ave.
New York, NY 10011

Show Business News
1301 Broadway
New York, NY 10036

Standard & Poor's Industry Surveys
Leisure-Time Current Analysis
300 W. Chestnut St.
Ephrata, PA 17522

Television Quarterly
National Academy of Television Arts
   and Sciences
110 W. 57th St.
New York, NY 10019

Television/Radio Age
1270 Avenue of the Americas
New York, NY 10010

Variety
154 W. 46th St.
New York, NY 10036

View
150 E. 58th St.
New York, NY 10155

Annotated and Selected Bibliography

The following books and periodicals are useful for examining different aspects of network television programming. We have included texts and reference directories that might provide you with additional information about the theory and practice of American television.

BOOKS

Barnouw, Erik. *Tube of Plenty: The Evolution of American Television*. New York: Oxford University Press, 1982. A history of the development of television, based on Barnouw's three-volume history of broadcasting in America.

Bedell, Sally. *Up the Tube: Primetime TV and the Silverman Years*. New York: The Viking Press, 1981. An investigative look at network programming activities and competition during Fred Silverman's reign as network programming chief.

Blum, Richard A. *Television Writing: From Concept to Contract*. Rev. ed. Boston: Focal Press (Butterworth Publishers), 1984. A comprehensive guide to program development theories and practices for writers of comedy, drama, and specials. Includes sample presentations, script formats, and marketplace analysis.

———. *American Film Acting: The Stanislavski Heritage*. Ann Arbor, Michigan: UMI Research Press, 1984. A survey of method acting techniques from stage to film, including analyses of tools for character development.

Bohn, Thomas, and Richard Stromgren. *Light and Shadows: A History of Motion Pictures*. New York: Alfred Publishing, 1975. A comprehensive history of cinema from its inception to the late twentieth century.

Brooks, Tim, and Earle Marsh. *The Complete Directory of Primetime Network TV Shows: 1946–Present.* Rev. ed. New York: Ballantine Books, 1981. A historical directory of primetime programs, including names, credits, and content of shows.

Brown, Les. *Encyclopedia of Television.* New York: Zoetrope, 1982. Analysis of network programming in the 1970s, including facts on content, individuals, and economics. This is a revision of the *New York Times Encyclopedia of Television.*

———. *Television: The Business Behind the Box.* New York: Harcourt Brace Jovanovich/Harvest, 1971. Informative account of programming practices, conflicts, and policy deliberations at the networks during the 1970–1971 television season.

Cantor, Muriel G. *The Hollywood TV Producer: His Work and His Audience.* New York: Basic Books, 1972. Sociological study of the primetime workplace based on eighty interviews with television producers.

Clift, Charles, III, and Archie Greer, eds. *Broadcasting Programming: The Current Perspective.* Washington, D.C.: University Press of America. Annual reprint of professional and academic articles on primetime programming schedules, ratings, and other programming concerns (such as local programming, public broadcasting, broadcast regulation, and lobby groups).

Eastman, Susan T., Sydney W. Head, and Lewis Klein, eds. *Broadcast/Cable Programming: Strategies and Practices.* 2d ed. Belmont, California: Wadsworth Publishing, 1985. Informative text with chapters by programmers in various areas, including primetime, nonprimetime, affiliated stations, independent stations, cable television, radio, and public broadcasting.

Eliot, Marc. *Televisions: One Season in American Television.* New York: St. Martin's Press, 1983. A look at the activities and strategies behind programming of the 1981–1982 television season.

Gianakos, Larry J. *Television Drama Series Programming: A Comprehensive Chronicle 1975–1980.* Metuchen, New Jersey: Scarecrow Press, 1981. A historical listing of network television dramatic shows, with dates of broadcast, cast lists, and cross-referenced information. Earlier editions cover earlier years.

Gitlin, Todd. *Inside Prime Time.* New York: Pantheon, 1983. A behind-the-scenes look at network programming, based on interviews with many executives, creators, and agents.

Gomery, Douglas. *The Hollywood Studio System.* New York: St. Martin's Press, 1986. A thorough history of the American film industry during the Golden Age, including descriptions of major studios and bibliographic sources.

Grote, David. *The End of Comedy: The Sitcom and the Comedic Tradition.* Hamden, Connecticut: Shoe String Press, 1983. An academic survey of the history of comedy and its evolution in network television programming.

Head, Sydney W., and Christopher H. Sterling. *Broadcasting in America: A Survey of Electronic Media.* 5th ed. Boston: Houghton-Mifflin, 1986. A detailed review of the evolution of broadcasting, with analyses of major developments in programming, technology, economics, effects, and controls.

Knight, Arthur. *The Liveliest Art: A Panoramic History of the Movies.* New York: Macmillan, 1957. A classic history of the motion picture industry from the late nineteeth century to mid-twentieth century.

Kolker, Robert P. *A Cinema of Loneliness: Penn, Kubrick, Coppola, Scorsese, Altman.* New York: Oxford University Press, 1980. An informative investigation into contemporary film theory and practice.

Levinson, Richard, and William Link. *Stay Tuned: An Inside Look at the Making of Prime-Time Television.* New York: St. Martin's Press, 1981. Creative activities and management obstacles encountered in developing specific series and television films for the networks.

Lichty, Lawrence W., and Malachi C. Topping. *American Broadcasting: A Source Book on the History of Radio and Television.* New York: Hastings House, 1975. A compilation of facts, statistics, and readings concerning all aspects of broadcasting, including network programming.

Metz, Robert. *CBS: Reflections in a Bloodshot Eye.* Chicago: Playboy Press, 1975. Informal history of people and events behind the CBS network.

Meyers, Richard. *TV Detectives.* San Diego, California: A.S. Barnes & Co., 1981. Informal history of the television detective genre.

Miller, Merle, and Evan Rhodes. *Only You Dick Daring: How to Write One Television Script and Make $50,000,000.* New York: William Sloan Associates, 1964. A classic anecdotal account of how a pilot project is developed, modified, and aborted.

Morgenstern, Steve, ed. *Inside the TV Business.* New York: Sterling, 1979. Different chapters by professionals in network television.

Newcomb, Horace, and Robert S. Alley. *The Producer's Medium: Conversations with Creators of American TV.* New York: Oxford University Press, 1983. Interesting compilation of interviews with eight successful producers of primetime network shows.

Nielsen, A. C., & Co. *The Television Audience.* Northbrook, Illinois: A. C. Nielsen & Co. An annual update of programming trends and viewer preferences published by the Nielsen marketing research company.

Paley, William S. *As It Happened: A Memoir.* New York: Doubleday, 1979. An autobiography of one of the pioneer network leaders. Paley recounts the development and scheduling strategies for classic network primetime shows.

Shanks, Robert. *The Cool Fire: How to Make It in Television.* New York: Norton, 1976. Informal rundown of the network television industry, from program development to production.

Sklar, Robert. *Prime-Time America: Life on and Behind the Television Screen.* New York: Oxford University Press, 1980. An informal critical overview of primetime television program content.

Steinberg, Cobbett. *TV Facts.* New York: Facts on File, Inc., 1980. Full compendium of facts and figures about the history of television, replete with statistics and directories compiled from a wide range of sources.

Webster, James. *Audience Research.* Washington, D.C.: National Association of Broadcasters, 1983. Basic survey of audience research methodology.

Whitfield, Steve, and Gene Roddenberry. *The Making of Star Trek.* New York: Ballantine Books, 1972. An informative account of how the classic science fiction series was created, from concept to sale and production. Original series presentation is included.

Wolper, David L., and Quincy Troupe. *The Inside Story of TV's 'Roots.'* New York: Warner Books, 1978. Behind-the-scenes account of the development, production, and network management strategies surrounding the miniseries "Roots."

INDUSTRY DIRECTORIES

Broadcasting Yearbook. 1735 DeSales St., N.W., Washington, DC 20036. Annual compilation of facts and figures about the television industry, including information about television stations across the country.

Cable File. Titsch Communications, 2500 Curtis St., Denver, CO 80217. Semiannual update of who's who in pay and basic cable programming.

Cable TV Program Data Book. Kagan & Associates, 26386 Carmel Rancho Lane, Carmel, CA 93923. Another semiannual directory for cable television program services.

Pacific Coast Directory. 6331 Hollywood Blvd., Hollywood, CA 90028. Quarterly directory of producers, agents, advertising agencies, and television stations.

Ross Reports. Television Index, Inc., 150 Fifth Ave., New York, NY 10011. Regular updates on casting, producing, and programming activities.

Television Factbook. 1836 Jefferson Place, N.W., Washington, DC 20036. Annual directory of contacts encompassing the entire industry, including independent producers, networks, stations, and cable companies.

Index